THE EVOLUTION OF AN IDEA

The MIT Press, the ☰MiTeenPress colophon, and MITeen Press are trademarks of
The MIT Press, a department of the Massachusetts Institute of Technology, and
used under license from The MIT Press. The colophon and MITeen are registered
in the US Patent and Trademark Office.

First edition 2024

Library of Congress Catalog Card Number pending
ISBN 978-1-5362-2294-4

24 25 26 27 28 29 CCP 10 9 8 7 6 5 4 3 2 1

Printed in Shenzhen, Guangdong, China

This book was typeset in Alegreya and Candara.

MITeen Press
an imprint of Candlewick Press
99 Dover Street
Somerville, Massachusetts 02144

miteenpress.com
candlewick.com

DISCOVERING LIFE'S STORY

VOLUME TWO

THE EVOLUTION OF AN IDEA

JOY HAKIM

≡MiTeenPress

Contents

An Age of Enlightenment and Evolution

Starting in 1751, a Frenchman named Denis Diderot publishes a sprawling series of books attempting to detail all the world's scientific, artistic, and technological knowledge. He titles the series the *Encyclopedia* and says the books, which he cowrites with other authors, are intended to change the way people think.

The title page of Diderot's original Encyclopedia

For Diderot, writing has been dangerous. He was imprisoned by French authorities for previous works. But Diderot is convinced of the power of words based on informed research; he is determined to use them to advance knowledge, no matter what kings or clergy think. "All things must be examined, debated, investigated without exception and without regard for anyone's feelings," he writes.

Also in 1751, a Swedish naturalist named Carl Linnaeus says that "in natural science the elements of truth ought to be confirmed by observation." Those words help give birth to a new age of organized thinking.

A bust of Denis Diderot by the French sculptor Jean-Antoine Houdon

This period of time will be known as the Enlightenment (or sometimes the Age of Reason). It began in the late seventeenth century and will continue through the eighteenth. In this age, experiments and observations are understood as essential if science is to advance beyond hypothesis. And that's not all; the very ways people perceive the world around them will be reconsidered.

"Dare to Know!"

That credo is used by Immanuel Kant, a German philosopher, to sum up the Enlightenment. Kant writes that enlightenment for an individual means learning to think for oneself. It means growing beyond an immaturity whose "cause lies not in lack of understanding, but in lack of resolve and courage to use it without guidance from another." He tells his readers to "have courage to use your own understanding!" Bear in mind that this admonition comes at a time when many of his fellow Europeans turn to the church or the monarch for their beliefs.

A portrait of the philosopher Immanuel Kant by Johann Gottlieb Becker

While this invigorated thinking is taking hold, there is a new global awareness, a new sharing of ideas, and increased travel among the continents. In cities around the world, thinkers are building on Enlightenment ideas in different ways and then sharing those ideas.

News from Asia floods back to Europe from missionaries and traders. According to a modern German historian, Jürgen Osterhammel, "Around the mid-eighteenth century, the public in France or Germany was better informed about China than about many countries on Europe's periphery."

A British philosopher, John Locke, has ideas that help lay the groundwork for democratic revolutions in America and France. Locke says that "all men by nature are equal" and have a right to their own life, liberty, and property. Jean-Jacques Rousseau, a French philosopher, says, "Man was born free; and everywhere he is in chains."

Such thinking inspires Thomas Jefferson, Benjamin Franklin, and others to seek independence for the British colonies in North America and forge what will become a new and rebellious nation.

Theirs are revolutionary ideas, but note the use of the words *man* and *men* when there is talk of rights. This is not an age of equal opportunity for women, although a few do make their voices heard. In France, a butcher's daughter, Olympe de Gouges, becomes a playwright. In 1791, she writes the *Declaration of the Rights of Woman and of the [Female] Citizen*. De Gouges has patterned her work after the *Declaration of the Rights of Man and of the [Male] Citizen*, written by the Marquis de Lafayette and others and adopted by France's National Constituent Assembly in 1789.

This painting by John Trumbull depicts the drafted Declaration of Independence being presented to the Continental Congress; it includes portraits of forty-two of the fifty-six signers.

This painting by Jean-Victor Schnetz depicts a scene from the July Revolution of 1830, part of the unrest that followed the French Revolution of 1789. It captures both the drama and the violence of France's fight for citizens' rights.

France's *Declaration of the Rights of Man,* published in 1789, declares that "men are born and remain free and equal in rights," an idea that becomes a cornerstone of the bloody French Revolution, which claims the heads of both Queen Marie Antoinette and her husband, King Louis XVI.

De Gouges makes her feelings clear in her own declaration: Women have a right to citizenship that is equal to men's, she says. At a time when men control their wives' property, she says that in marriage, men and women should share property. Then she goes further in other published work; a fierce abolitionist, she writes a play attacking slavery. She is horrified that Europeans are selling people "like cows at market," she will write.

De Gouges's ideas may seem like common sense today, but in the eighteenth century, they are dangerous. Like many people who get involved in politics and speak their mind during the French Revolution, she eventually falls out of favor and is tried for treason and executed.

Ideas about natural rights as embodied in the American and French Revolutions spark movements elsewhere. In their own revolution, for instance, fought from 1791 to 1804, enslaved people in the French colony of Saint Domingue revolt and reclaim their country for themselves. The new sovereign nation is named Haiti. Although this revolution is led by people of color and ends slavery in the colony, this broader definition of who is endowed with natural rights is not adopted in either America or France. And even in Haiti, as a price for

Olympe de Gouges; portrait by Alexander Kucharsky

A scene from the Haitian Revolution, a rebellion against French colonizers

Mary Wollstonecraft, who is British, also believes that women are men's equals and should be treated as such in both their education and place in society. She makes that case in *A Vindication of the Rights of Woman*, published in 1792. Her daughter Mary Wollstonecraft Shelley (who marries the poet and philosopher Percy Bysshe Shelley) will find her own way to be heard—writing a number of novels, including an enduring classic, *Frankenstein*, about an eight-foot-tall creature built from body parts.

John Opie's portrait of Mary Wollstonecraft

Mary Shelley

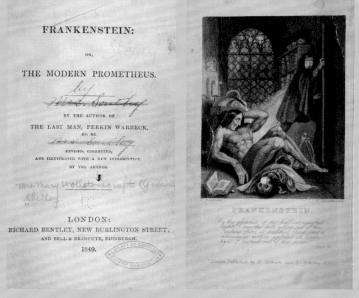

Pages from an early edition of Mary Shelley's Frankenstein

ensuring peace, the government will be saddled for generations with debts to those who held people in bondage.

During these times of political upheavals, there is also revolution afoot in science.

For much of European history, there has been a clear order and hierarchy of beings, with God at the top. The prevailing view is that there have been no major changes in life since humans were created. Most people believe life is controlled by divine forces beyond human understanding. Evolution and extinction have no place in this model.

But cracks have appeared in this foundational knowledge. If each animal is perfectly made to suit its environment, why do similar environments hold dramatically different

A late sixteenth-century engraving called The Sixth Day: The Creation of Animals, Adam and Eve

creatures? Why has Mary Anning, the British Enlightenment fossil hunter, found seaside bones so large that they could belong to no living species? Is it possible that some life-forms have gone extinct? Almost no one believes that (although it is true), but some geological findings, uncovered in layers of ancient rock, seem to have been left behind by creatures no longer found on Earth.

New ideas about how life changes over time battle against the commonly held belief that all species are as they have been since creation. This leads to fierce differences of opinion. A French professor, Jean-Baptiste Lamarck, comes up with a radical idea. He says that animals do change, that they adjust to their environment, acquire new traits, and that this change can eventually lead to new species. Lamarck's scientific rival, Baron Georges Cuvier, studies the fossil record and claims that life sometimes changes abruptly in response to catastrophic events such as earthquakes but not gradually, as Lamarck believes. This becomes a big debate among those who think scientifically, a group that is coming to include more and more people.

An 1839 painting titled Man of Science

Scientific exploration has become a popular pastime for the well-heeled and the intellectually curious, men and women alike. Now many people are searching for clues as to how life works. They hike up mountains and along streams. Some study the heavens, trying to figure out our place in the universe. Others study animals, shells, and fossils, often documenting what they discover.

This age of popular scientific exploration sets the stage for two Englishmen, Charles Darwin and Alfred Russel Wallace, who will each develop

The listeners in this 1768 etching, A Philosopher Giving a Lecture on the Orrery, *range in age from young to old. An orrery is a model of the solar system.*

a new and startling idea about life based on the concept that life-forms have changed, or evolved, and continue to do so. Some will recognize the importance of this joint discovery; many will be dismayed. Few will understand its far-reaching consequences. Given time, the evolutionary idea—that life-forms change over time—will shake the foundations of established thinking. It will transform human understanding of our place in the universe. ■

The Organization Man

A portrait of Swedish botanist Carl Linnaeus, who came up with a naming system for plants and animals

It's time for us to get organized. No, seriously, we *really* need to get organized. Earth's creatures are a sprawling jumble, and no one quite understands how they relate to one another. There are finches and crows, turtles and elephants, dogs and cats, and different variations of each. Can anyone make sense of it all? Who will take on this daunting task?

Enter Carl Linnaeus (1707–1778), a man of modest means and the son of a Swedish clergyman. Inspired by his father's love of gardening and thanks to an influential schoolteacher, Linnaeus learns to love botany, or the study of plants. Initially he

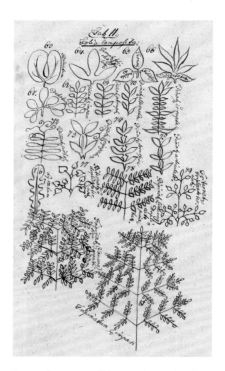

A page from one of Linnaeus's notebooks

chooses to make a living as a medical doctor, but botany is his true passion. In 1735, at age twenty-eight, while studying in the Netherlands, he publishes *Systema Naturae*, or *The System of Nature*.

This book creates a hierarchy of life, starting at the top with two kingdoms—plants and animals—and then dividing life-forms into smaller groups whose members are linked by similar characteristics. It's a linear progression into ever-more-specific sets, each nesting inside the last. The geographic equivalent would be classifying someone as living in the universe, in the Milky Way galaxy, on Earth, in the United States, in the state of Virginia, in Virginia Beach, in a house on Ocean Avenue.

Linnaeus will update his great work throughout his life. His first version is eleven pages long. His final edition stretches to three thousand pages. He applies organized scientific thinking to life on Earth. As one biographer will say of him: "God created, Linnaeus organized."

The two Linnaean kingdoms seem broad enough at the time to hold all of life. (Minerals are considered non-life and handed over to geologists.) A modified version of the organizational system remains in use today, using classifications starting with domain and narrowing to kingdom, phylum, class, order, family, genus, and species. Genus and species are given as shorthand: Lions are *Panthera leo*. Great white sharks are *Carcharodon carcharias*. And we are *Homo sapiens*.

Linnaeus even uses his classification system to settle some personal grievances. He names a genus of foul-smelling plants *Siegesbeckia*, after a rival botanist named Johann Georg Siegesbeck, who is critical of Linnaeus's work. A species of beetle is named after a former student who fell out of favor. Best not to provoke Linnaeus.

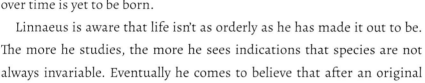

Most people in the eighteenth and early-nineteenth centuries think that life-forms have not changed since life was first created all at once. Linnaeus doesn't challenge that idea; he just attempts to organize life as it exists. Evolutionary biology and its understanding that life-forms change over time is yet to be born.

Linnaeus is aware that life isn't as orderly as he has made it out to be. The more he studies, the more he sees indications that species are not always invariable. Eventually he comes to believe that after an original creation, new species can arise as mixtures or hybrids. He even theorizes that plant species sometimes change by adapting to their environments. He is both a man of his time and someone who manages to question accepted ideas.

Linnaeus's drawing of Siegesbeckia

Not all of Linnaeus's work demonstrates scientific rigor. He classifies humans into regional subgroups and assigns racist stereotypes that have nothing to do with science and everything to do with preconceived notions of what people around the world are like. His work will begin a noxious and false strain of thought asserting that certain races are inherently superior to others, which will persist among academics in the field of biology. These ideas will have wide-ranging, and often deadly, political and cultural influence.

Today his failings are acknowledged. London's Linnean Society, the world's oldest society of natural history, takes its name from the famous Swede. But the society has been frank in its assessment of his faults, writing that "one of the origins of scientific

A Circumnavigator in Disguise

Jeanne Baret (1740–1807) is born in France to a poor family. She has an early curiosity about plants and learns to identify them and their medicinal properties, developing a gift for botany. She meets and falls in love with Philibert Commerson, a well-known naturalist living in Paris, who is a friend of Carl Linnaeus. In 1766, France's Louis-Antoine de Bougainville, an explorer and sea captain, is planning a voyage around the world in search of lands little known to Europeans. He asks Linnaeus for guidance, and Linnaeus suggests that Bougainville bring Commerson along to collect plants. Commerson agrees but wants Baret to accompany him and work alongside him. In France in this era, however, women aren't allowed on government ships. So Baret wears sailor's clothes and pretends to be a man.

A portrait of Jeanne Baret dressed as a sailor, made after her death

They sail south from France, around the southern tip of South America, into the Pacific Ocean, stop on the island of Tahiti, and then sail on to Papua New Guinea. Baret and Commerson collect and catalog plants from around the world, including a gorgeous colorful vine that gets named bougainvillea, after the ship's captain. But Baret's gender is eventually discovered, and she and Commerson are dropped off at Mauritius, an island in the Indian Ocean that was then a French colony. Baret and Commerson remain together on the island. Years later, after Commerson's death, Baret returns to France. She becomes the first woman known to have circumnavigated the Earth.

racism can be traced to Linnaeus's work on the classification of man, which had devastating and far-reaching consequences for humanity."

His work does lead to real revolutions in scientific thinking. When Linnaeus classifies humans as a species of animal, it is a bold move, upsetting to many who believe that humans are unique. Many also think that life's divisions are just as they were when

Linnaeus goes beyond naming. An unexplored botanical theory fascinates the vibrant Swede: it's the idea that most plants have sexual organs—stamens and pistils—that are basic to reproduction. He compares plant reproduction to human weddings in florid writing that is controversial in his day.

An eighteenth-century illustration of the flowering and fruiting stages of the fig

Earth was first created. For those who don't believe that the traits and characteristics of Earth's inhabitants have been changing over time, the idea of evolution makes no sense.

In a private letter to a good friend and fellow naturalist, Johann Gmelin, on January 14, 1747, Linnaeus uses the term *differentia* to mean a set of characteristics that make one species distinct from another, writing, "I ask you and the whole world for a generic differentia between man and ape which conforms to the principles of natural history, I certainly know of none."

Linnaeus speaks that idea quietly. He knows that his discovery of a biological relationship among all forms of life challenges long-held religious beliefs. Linnaeus is onto something, but he realizes that saying too much about the mechanics of life can make people angry. There will be more controversy ahead for his scientific successors. As he tells his friend: "If I were to call man ape or vice versa, I should bring down all the theologians on my head. But perhaps I should still do it according to the rules of science." ∎

Big Thinking with Buffon

02

Buffon's work on the discovery of deep time is of monumental importance. His extension for the age of the earth to 74,832 years was a giant leap beyond Bishop Ussher's biblical calculation of 4004 B.C. for the creation. In private Buffon estimated an age of three million years or more, possibly infinity, but did not want to shock his readers and so stuck with the more conservative estimate. Yet he confessed, "The more we extend the time, the closer to the truth."

—Michael Shermer

The grand workman of nature is Time.

—Georges-Louis Leclerc, comte de Buffon

The Comte de Buffon, a wealthy French landowner and naturalist with a dim view of America

While Carl Linnaeus is trying to figure out names for all of life's forms, his French contemporary Georges-Louis Leclerc, the Comte de Buffon, or Count of Buffon, turns up his aristocratic nose at the Swede's work and does his own classifying. Buffon considers himself the greatest biologist of the day. When Linnaeus hears Buffon's criticism, he once again uses his scientific naming system to get even: he names a type of weed *Buffonia*. It's a weed that stinks.

Buffon (1707–1788), born the same year as Linnaeus, probably never takes time to sniff his namesake flower. Today we might call him a workaholic. His father buys the village of Buffon for him, which is how Leclerc eventually becomes the Comte de Buffon. And he inherits a fortune as a young man when his mother dies.

Buffon has the means to live a life of indolent ease; instead he gets up at five every morning, often working a fourteen-hour day managing his properties, undertaking scientific research, and writing books and papers—all while doing his day job as keeper of France's magnificent royal garden, called the Jardin des Plantes, which hosts public

The Grand Gallery of Evolution in Paris, part of the Jardin des Plantes

lectures and other events. He spends almost forty years, from 1749 to 1788, researching, writing, and publishing a thirty-six-volume encyclopedia of nature, *Histoire naturelle* (*Natural History*). That masterwork becomes an eighteenth-century must-have for anyone interested in the natural world. Nine more of Buffon's volumes will be published after he dies. According to twentieth-century biologist Ernst Mayr, Buffon's encyclopedia was read "by every educated person in Europe." Mayr might have added "in the United States too." Thomas Jefferson's copy can be seen today at the Library of Congress.

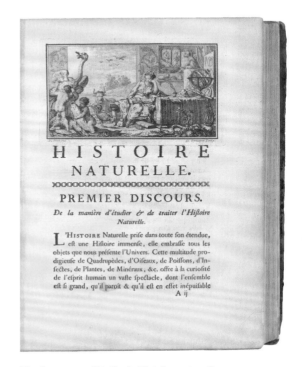

The first page of Buffon's Histoire naturelle

Buffon's timing is excellent. The second half of the eighteenth century is a terrific period for big thinkers. Before 1750, books are very expensive and not distributed widely. In Europe, families that include a reader usually own a Bible and, if they are lucky, maybe one or two other books. After 1750, as the book industry expands, the reading public does too.

City folks, who are more likely to go to school, are now able to gorge on written materials. In big cities like London, hawkers sell newspapers on the streets. Papers are also distributed by shops set up by female entrepreneurs known as "mercury women" because they sell newspapers, pamphlets, and books that often need to be marketed quickly. Some hawkers even start taking newspapers from house to house, giving each family a set amount of time to read before passing the paper on to the next subscriber. In France, the literacy rate doubles in just a few years.

By the eighteenth century, London has thousands of coffeehouses, where people exchange books, broadsheets, pamphlets, journals—and ideas—as they sip their brew, and Germany has a similar coffeehouse culture. Paris has cafés. These open meeting places are called "talking shops." The shops are open to both women and men of all classes and professions, laying foundations for democracies to come. Buffon is a kind of celebrity hero in this intellectually emerging world.

In volume 1 of his *Histoire*, Buffon suggests that the Earth is very old. Most people believe that when the Bible says there were seven days of creation, that means seven actual days. Buffon says they can be considered as seven epochs, with a biblical day being many thousands of years long. That thought is too much for French religious authorities. Buffon is forced to publish a recantation (it comes in volume 4 of *Histoire*). His books are banned and burned by Catholic authorities. A few scholarly Jesuits read them anyway. Buffon has planted an idea that will grow among a significant part of the reading public.

Then Buffon takes it a step further and sets out to find out just how old the Earth actually is. How can he do that?

A 1792 French etching called A Patriot's Coffee House

He knows that the Earth is composed of metals and minerals and that iron is an important component. He assumes that the Earth was once in a molten state and then cooled. To determine Earth's age, Buffon conducts experiments on how quickly iron cools and then makes estimates about the length of time the Earth has been cooling.

He has ten iron bullets made, one that is half an inch (1.3 centimeters) in diameter, another an inch (2.5 centimeters) in diameter, on up to one that is five inches (12.7 centimeters) in diameter. He brings the bullets to a white heat, considers them as they cool, and comes to this conclusion: "Instead of 50,000 years, which Newton assigns for the earth to cool to the present temperature, it would require 42,964 years, 221 days, to cool only to the point where it ceased to burn."

Molten iron at an iron-casting factory

Starting there, Buffon figures out that Earth must be at least 75,000 years old and maybe as old as 168,000 years. This is a huge insight at a time when most English churchgoers accept the well-regarded bishop James Ussher's biblical interpretation of Earth's age as just six thousand years. Later, thinking about England's chalk cliffs, Buffon realizes that they are built of layers of marine life, and that it would take eons for shells to turn into chalk. Buffon theorizes that the Earth might even be as old as ten *million* years.

Buffon's next step is to consider the creation of life itself. According to Ernst Mayr, "He was the first person to discuss a large number of evolutionary problems, problems that prior to Buffon had not been raised by anybody." Buffon believes it possible that life first arose through natural biological processes; he's sometimes

How old is the Earth? Buffon is off by a few billion years. His estimate is better than what most thinkers of his time believe, but it is still much too low. The Earth is actually a bit more than 4.5 *billion* years old.

called a founder of evolutionary science. That science is built on the idea that life-forms have changed over time and continue to do so. Buffon attempts to explain scientifically why and how that is the case.

Buffon notes that different regions of the Earth produce different plants and animals, even if their environments are similar. That concept is known today as Buffon's Law.

Buffon is way ahead of most of his contemporaries when he sees a link between all of life. He says, "There is no absolute essential and general difference between animals and vegetables, but that nature descends, by degrees imperceptibly from an animal which is the most perfect, to that which is the least, and from the latter to the vegetable." He also floats an idea that will resurface in the twenty-first century: "Lines of separation do not exist in nature; there are beings which are neither animals, vegetables, nor minerals."

An image from Buffon's Histoire naturelle

There are several things Buffon doesn't get right. He believes life started with a kind of perfection and then began a downhill slide. For example, he sees the elephant of his day as smaller (and inferior) to what he believes was the original creation: the ancient mastodon. When he notes the similarities between apes and humans, he considers the possibility of a common ancestry (apes being degraded humans).

Buffon is trying to find his way in an unexplored field. While his ideas on how nature's changes happen are way off, just considering the possibility of natural processes and the great expanse of time they would need to occur takes a huge leap of mind. For many, his mental leaps are heresy, but they introduce a big concept to a broad audience.

Buffon writes that life may have first appeared on Earth in a cold region, probably Siberia (which is part of Russia). Russia's ruler, Catherine the Great, is delighted to have her land get this attention. She sends Buffon gold medals and a snuffbox decorated with diamonds.

An engraving of Catherine the Great, empress of Russia

Some of Buffon's theories are marked by racist ideas that will play out into the future. He believes that white Europeans represent an ideal human and people with darker skin in other parts of the world are "degenerate," or inferior, versions. Such ideas will be expanded on by others and will eventually feed murderous ideologies like Nazism.

When it comes to the Americas, Buffon is dismissive. He falsely believes that a humid climate in America has led to a lack of large and powerful creatures. He characterizes Indigenous people of the Americas as less virile than their European counterparts, describing them as newcomers on the human scene who are degraded examples of perfect humans, which to him means Europeans.

Buffon is letting his own prejudice taint his scientific thinking and dealing in hearsay, or unverified information and rumor, instead of firsthand knowledge. He has never met an Indigenous American. Europeans who have actually visited America have noted the health and vigor of the Indigenous people. But prejudice is built on ignorance.

When Buffon writes of the marsh odors, the humidity, and the dense forests of the American continent, he relies on secondhand reports. Here's a bit from his *Histoire naturelle*:

> *In America, therefore, animated Nature is weaker, less active, and more circumscribed in the variety of her productions; . . . the numbers of species is not only fewer, but . . . in general, all the animals are much smaller than those of the Old Continent.*

Others will pick up and expand these ideas. Cornelius de Pauw, a Dutch clergyman, and Guillaume Raynal, a Jesuit priest and popular author, will argue in their writings that the climate of America will lead to a degeneration in the nature of white colonists as well as Native Americans. None of these men have been to America.

After reading Buffon, the US minister to France, Thomas Jefferson, writes to New Hampshire's governor, John Sullivan, asking him to send the skeleton, horns, and hide of a bull moose to establish the preeminence of American animals. Sullivan dispatches a team of soldiers to the New Hampshire woods. After two weeks of tracking, they find a moose and shoot it, but it lacks big horns. Before shipping it to France, they attach a rack of large antlers that belonged to a stag or an elk in place of its original horns.

Clashing Worldviews

By the eighteenth century, America's Indigenous peoples are losing the land that they live on as the number of colonists grows and the European population spreads.

For the newcomers, land ownership is a big thing. Most want to own a farm they can settle and work and pass on to their children and grandchildren. Indigenous peoples have a different view, often seeing themselves as custodians of the land rather than owners of it. To many Native Americans, the white world of land deeds and settlers threatens their way of life.

"Our land is more valuable than your money," Crowfoot, a chief of the Blackfeet tribe, will say in the 1800s.

It will last forever. It will not even perish by the flames of fire. As long as the sun shines and the waters flow, this land will be here to give life to men and animals. We cannot sell the lives of men and animals; therefore, we cannot sell this land. It was put here for us by the Great Spirit and we cannot sell it because it does not belong to us. You can count your money and burn it within the nod of a buffalo's head, but only the Great Spirit can count the grains of sand and the blades of grass of these plains.

Isapo-muxika, also known as Crowfoot

"Who in France, after all, would know?" modern author Bill Bryson writes in his retelling of the tale.

Then Jefferson writes a book, *Notes on the State of Virginia*, in good part to rebut the much-read Count Buffon. In his book, Jefferson goes on for page after page, with charts and passion, defending the virility of his nation, its people, and its animals. But like Linnaeus before him, he allows prejudices and stereotypes to distort his scientific thinking. According to the Thomas Jefferson Foundation, in his book he:

Thomas Jefferson, third president of the United States (from 1801 to 1809)

recorded information about the natural history, inhabitants, and political organization of Virginia, including his most extensive discussion of his views on race. Like many other 18th-century thinkers, Jefferson believed blacks were inferior to whites. He questioned whether their low status was due to inherent inferiority or to decades of degrading enslavement.

Still, during his lifetime, Jefferson champions many of the values that lie at the core of American democracy. As indicated on his gravestone, he wanted to be remembered for three things: that he was author of the Declaration of Independence, that he wrote a Virginia statute enshrining religious freedom, and that he founded the University of Virginia. But his racism cannot be overlooked or ignored. Nor can the fact that he enslaved hundreds of people in Virginia.

Buffon, convinced by Jefferson's argument and firsthand experience with life in America, agrees to revise his next printing, and he may mean to do so, but when he dies in 1788, he hasn't gotten to it. So Buffon's flawed book continues to influence readers.

Ben Franklin later arranges a dinner in Paris with the clergyman Guillaume Raynal, who believes Americans of all races are physically inferior to Europeans. Jefferson later describes what takes place in a letter, after being told about it by Franklin:

> *During the dinner Abbé Raynal got on his favorite theory of the degeneracy of animals, and even of man in America. . . . The doctor [Franklin] at length said, "We are one half Americans and one half French. . . . Let both parties rise, and we will see on which side nature degenerated."*

Now, it happens that all of Franklin's American dinner guests are tall and athletic. Jefferson continues with glee, "Those of the other side were remarkably diminutive." The point was made, but from today's perspective, the ridiculousness of this episode makes clear that science is a discipline still finding its way.

Even after he becomes president, Jefferson remains determined to rebut the ideas left behind by Buffon and show that animals in America can be gigantic. The moose is not enough. When he comes across huge bones, said to come from a giant creature called "the incognitum, or mammoth," he decides that finding one will put the matter of American inferiority to rest.

Woolly mammoths were largely extinct by about ten thousand years ago.

No one Jefferson knows has actually seen one of those woolly elephant-like creatures, but the president is sure living mammoths must be around somewhere. Like just about everyone else, he believes that the variety of life that inhabits the Earth is as it has always been. Since he doesn't believe species can go extinct, he is sure that mammoths must be wandering about in the vast western territory he has just purchased from France. In 1804, he sends Meriwether Lewis and William Clark out to explore the far west of the North American continent and gives them instructions to search for mammoths.

> *It is well known, that on the Ohio, and in many parts of America further north, tusks, grinders, and skeletons of unparalleled magnitude, are found in great numbers, some lying on the surface of the earth, and some a little below it. . . . But to whatever animal we ascribe these remains, it is certain that such a one has existed in America, and that it has been the largest of all terrestrial beings.*
>
> *—Thomas Jefferson*

They don't find any. Is it possible that some animals that once roamed the Earth no longer exist? Jefferson can't swallow that idea. "Such is the economy of nature," he writes, "that no instance can be produced, of her having permitted any one race of her animals to become extinct; of her having formed any link in her great work so weak as to be broken."

Jefferson is stating the widely held belief in a "Great Chain of Being," which holds that in our perfectly designed world, every living thing has its essential and ordered place in a greater whole. It's a concept that can be traced to Plato and Aristotle, and it was further developed in medieval religious thinking. The basic idea: all life fits into a hierarchy, with God on top, followed by angels, kings, princes and nobles, other humans, animals, trees, other plants, minerals, and, on the bottom, dirt. Neither extinction nor evolution fits that scheme.

Jefferson and many of his contemporaries are fascinated by the emerging world of science, but some things test their understanding. In 1807, at 6:30 on the morning of December 14, some meteorites fall from the sky in Connecticut. Jefferson, who is

In the early-morning hours of December 14, 1807, a Connecticut judge is out for a walk when he sees a fiery globe hurtling in the sky, followed a minute later by loud explosions. It is a meteorite, a rocky object in space that has broken up and fallen to earth.

Locals head for the meteorite's landing spot, in Weston, Connecticut, where they pick up and smash pieces of it, convinced that if it fell from the heavens, it must contain gold or silver (they are wrong). The largest remaining piece weighs about 36 pounds (16 kilograms).

The new nation has no experts on astronomy. Yale University's first science professor, Benjamin Silliman, hired in 1802, is a chemist and natural historian. When he gets a report of the fallen star, he sets out for Weston, where he talks to eyewitnesses and studies pieces of the meteorite; then he writes a scientific report about what he finds.

A piece of the Weston meteorite

still president, is no fool. But when he reads a report on the meteorites from a pair of Yale College professors, he laughs. The president, who hasn't stopped searching for mammoths, says, "It is easier to believe that two Yankee professors could lie than to admit that stones could fall from heaven."

But stones did drop from the heavens (maybe from a comet). Our universe is not static.

Things change. That idea of change over time, which is the evolutionary idea, will face resistance in Western culture, which has long believed in a static world that is basically unchanged since its creation. ■

The Life of the Lunaticks

03

The Lunar men are different—together they nudge their whole society and culture over the threshold of the modern, tilting it irrevocably away from old patterns of life towards the world we know today.

—Jenny Uglow

The improved steam engine marks the first significant increase in the power available to humans for many millennia. . . . With the introduction of steam power, then of electricity and oil, human societies began at last to draw on the huge sources of energy locked up in the inorganic world.

—David Christian

An 1889 oil painting of James Watt's workroom by the artist Jonathon Pratt

Officially, a group of innovative businessmen and inventors who meet regularly in England's Midlands form the Lunar Society of Birmingham. But they call themselves Lunaticks (or sometimes Lunarticks). And why not? These men have a sense of humor, and they are attempting to change their world. They are not only birthing the Industrial Revolution; they are questioning established thinking and having a great time doing so. They are also getting rich.

Perhaps because they live in the Midlands, rather than in London or Oxford or Cambridge, they feel free to think and do as they want. In this dynamic time, the British middle class is expanding; the Lunaticks will help lead the way.

Once a month they meet for "a little philosophical laughing." In other words, when they get together, along with discussing big ideas, they tell jokes and adventure stories—and they keep at it for thirty years. Their laughter begins at two in the afternoon on the Monday nearest the full moon; it goes on and on through dinner and beyond. Riding a horse home late at night is safest when the moon is full and bright.

Josiah Wedgwood, a social reformer who creates elegant pottery, is a founding member of the Lunaticks. "I hate piddling," Wedgwood writes, and he further says that he will "surprise *the World* with wonders." And he does. As the queen's official potter, he carries out experiment after experiment to perfect his pottery. It takes five thousand tries before Wedgwood develops an unglazed and flat finish, lacking in shine, creating a style of porcelain known as jasperware that will become famous for its elegance.

A late eighteenth-century Wedgwood vase housed at the Art Institute of Chicago

Erasmus Darwin (1731–1802), the grandfather of Charles Darwin and a man with a big personality who is another founder of the group, apologizes for missing a Monday get-together, saying in a note: "Lord! what invention, what wit, what rhetorick, metaphysical, mechanical and pyrotechnical will be on the wing, bandied like a shuttlecock from one to another of your troop of philosophers."

Matthew Boulton, a manufacturer and businessman who helps pioneer mass production, is also a founding member. He backs a new and more efficient steam engine designed by another Lunatick, James Watt. After author James Boswell calls on Boulton, he writes in his journal, "I shall never forget Mr Bo[u]lton's expression to me: 'I sell here, Sir, what all of the world desires to have,—Power.'"

It is that power, and the understanding that it is a marketable commodity, that makes the Industrial Revolution truly revolutionary. These Lunaticks help make it happen.

Other members include Joseph Priestley (a radical preacher who discovers oxygen), Dr. William Small (who has been to the wilds of Virginia, where he mentored Thomas Jefferson at the College of William and Mary), James Keir (who creates a lucrative metal alloy), and William Herschel (who discovers the planet Uranus).

The core group of Lunaticks share thoughts with intellectual leaders in Edinburgh, including economist Adam Smith, poet Robert Burns, chemist Joseph Black, and geologist James Hutton. "The linking of science to philosophy and literature was typical of the ethos of contemporary Scotland," writes Jenny Uglow, a modern writer, in her book *The Lunar Men*. She

The eighteenth-century English industrialist Matthew Boulton

The Scottish inventor and engineer James Watt

A Candle in a Jar

Joseph Priestley knows that a mouse, or any animal, placed in a sealed jar will soon die. Will a plant put in a jar outlast a mouse? He conducts an experiment to find out. The answer is yes, the plant lives longer than the mouse. Next, Priestley puts a candle in a jar with a plant, and the candle soon goes out. Twenty-seven days later, the plant is still alive, and Priestley relights the candle using mirrors and sunlight. The plant, he realizes, has created the oxygen that is needed for the candle to burn.

Yes! Priestley has discovered oxygen. His friend Ben Franklin, who is fascinated by science, understands the significance of this experiment. He uses the findings to extol the value of trees, writing to Priestley:

> I hope this will give some check to the rage of destroying trees that grow near houses, which has accompanied our late improvements in gardening, from an opinion of their being unwholesome. I am certain, from long observation, that there is nothing unhealthy in the air of woods.

Joseph Priestley, theologian and scientist

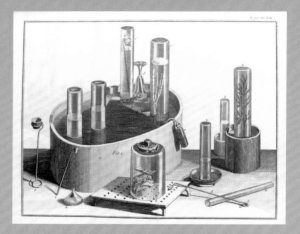

One of Priestley's experiments

adds, "At times it would seem as though Birmingham itself was an intellectual colony of Scotland."

But the Lunaticks are independent thinkers. Dedicated to capitalism, they nevertheless see themselves as revolutionaries. Among them, they will harness the power of electricity and steam, delve into experimental science, and build canals. Two centuries later, historian Jacob Bronowski writes of the Lunar Society, "What ran through it was a simple faith: the good life . . . must be based on material decency."

When Ben Franklin is in England, he attends Lunar Society meetings. Antoine Lavoisier (often called the "father of chemistry") sends letters to the members from France. Thomas Jefferson corresponds from America. The Lunaticks study Copernicus, Galileo, and Newton.

All the Lunaticks are big thinkers. But perhaps none more so than founding member Erasmus Darwin. A physician, poet, inventor, and botanist, Darwin helps translate the works of botany's organizing genius—Linnaeus—into English. When King George III (the one who loses thirteen colonies) asks Darwin to be royal physician, he politely declines. Darwin has a clientele of rich patients and needs no more. He also cares for the poor at no fee. Much of his time is spent in his carriage, going from patient to patient along rutted country roads. A letter addressed to "Dr. Darwin upon the road" will be delivered to him in his carriage.

That carriage is equipped with bookshelves, pen and paper, food, and a skylight cut into the roof. A saddle horse named Doctor is attached behind; if the carriage gets stuck in

Erasmus Darwin: scientist, abolitionist, grandfather of Charles

mud, Darwin can mount the horse and lose no time. It is in that swaying carriage that Erasmus Darwin writes much of the poetry that brings him popular fame.

Darwin has a limp from a childhood injury and a stammer. But he is hardly deterred. He becomes a successful physician and a popular poet of his day.

Among Darwin's inventions is a new kind of windmill and an innovative steering system for carriages that will influence automobiles years later. In an experiment, he coats plant leaves with oil, watches as the experimental plants die, then figures out that plants must breathe through tiny pores in the leaves (stomata). Inspired by his experiments, he pens a long poem, "The Loves of Plants."

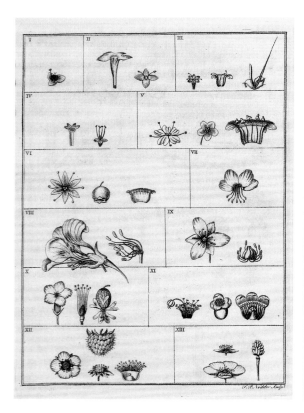
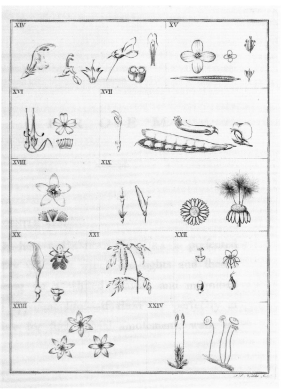

Illustrations from Erasmus Darwin's The Botanic Garden

An avid fossil digger, he pays attention when his friend geologist James Hutton studies rock layers. Hutton understands that he is seeing back through time when he examines layers of soil and rock, and he writes extensively on the topic.

As for Darwin, he dances to his own music. Perhaps it is the name he carries. His parents named him after Desiderius Erasmus, the great Renaissance humanist and Catholic priest who created controversy in his day when he attempted to marry religion and science, concepts that are often seen as incompatible.

The name is apt. Erasmus Darwin, amid all of his observations and experimenting, becomes obsessed with an idea that disturbs many of his contemporaries: the notion

Poet Samuel Taylor Coleridge doesn't agree with those who laud Erasmus Darwin as a poet. He can't stand Darwin's verse. (Coleridge's best-known poem is "The Rime of the Ancient Mariner," which includes the often-quoted lines "Water, water everywhere, / Nor any drop to drink.") Of Darwin's *The Botanic Garden*, he says, "I absolutely nauseate Darwin's poem," but he does admit that "Dr. Darwin possesses perhaps a greater range of knowledge than any man in Europe."

Samuel Taylor Coleridge, picky poet

that nature changes over time. The Lunaticks call it "evolutionism," "transmutation of species," and "developmentalism." Although they have no doubt that life has evolved and is still evolving, this is a controversial idea. Most mainstream thinkers, including most scholars, still believe in the Great Chain of Being concept, where each life-form is unique and not directly related to any other.

A depiction of the Great Chain of Being

Erasmus Darwin believes that life began in the water—many scientists today agree that life's origin was likely in the oceans—and though he often avoids directly spelling out his views, given how controversial they are, he is by no means entirely silent. Darwin even adopts a new coat of arms with scallop shells and a Latin phrase, *E conchis omnia*, which means "Everything from shells," a whimsical move that draws a reprimand from a local clergyman.

Not that Darwin literally believes that seashells specifically are the origin of life, but he rejects the thinking of the day: the Great Chain. For Darwin, the concept of change over time is a basic part of the life story. It emerges from his observations of plants, animals, and animal development. This is a far-out and unproven hypothesis, but Erasmus is sure of it.

As a doctor, Darwin has an interest in how babies form. He sets aside a chapter in his two-volume popular prose work titled *Zoonomia*, published in the 1790s, for the placenta, an organ that women's bodies—and those of other female mammals—create during pregnancy to feed fetuses in the womb and provide oxygen. He also closely examines embryos from various species and can see that life begins as a tiny mass of cells: "a living filament, with certain capabilities of irritation, sensation, volition, and association. . . . In some this filament . . . has acquired hands and fingers. . . . In others it has acquired claws or talons. . . . In others, toes with intervening web."

The title page of Erasmus Darwin's Zoonomia

How do filaments of cells know to turn into hands and not claws, or vice versa? And what explains an extra toe or other anomalies?

Darwin is struggling to figure that out. He accepts an idea of Lamarck's called "use and disuse." Under that theory, if someone, say a blacksmith, uses and builds up his arm muscles, those powerful arms may be passed on to his children. In *Zoonomia*, Darwin cites evidence that species change over time and asks:

> Would it be too bold to imagine, that in the great length of time, since the earth began to exist . . . that all warm-blooded animals have arisen from one living filament, which THE GREAT FIRST CAUSE endued with animality, with the power of acquiring new parts . . . and of delivering down those improvements by generation to its posterity, world without end?

In a poem in a later book, *The Temple of Nature*, he makes the case that modern life arose from tiny organisms:

> Organic Life beneath the shoreless waves
> Was born and nursed in Ocean's pearly caves;
> First forms minute, unseen by spheric glass,
> Move on the mud, or pierce the watery mass;

A Darwin Finds a Fossil

In 1718, Erasmus's father, Robert Darwin, who lives in the town of Elston, England, is shown a strange fossil embedded in stone. No one knows what the fossil is, although it seems to be some kind of life-form. (Much later, this rare fossil will be classified as a plesiosaur from the Jurassic period.) Robert Darwin sends the unusual stone to the Royal Society in London. As a thank-you, he is invited to a meeting, and there he meets the president of the Royal Society: Isaac Newton.

This is a big moment in Robert's life; he is fascinated by science and he understands that Newton is challenging traditional scientific ideas. Robert, who reads a lot, names his son after the famous Renaissance scholar. And Erasmus Darwin's son, another Robert Darwin, is a doctor who becomes very rich on investments. That Robert Darwin has two sons: he names one Erasmus, the other Charles.

Cast of a plesiosaur skeleton found in Somerset, England

These, as successive generations bloom,
New powers acquire, and larger limbs assume;
Whence countless groups of vegetation spring,
And breathing realms of fin, and feet, and wing.

These ideas *are* too bold, perhaps not for the Lunaticks, but for most others in the eighteenth and nineteenth centuries. Later, after the heady early years of the Industrial Revolution, evolution will become a touchy subject. So too are some of Erasmus Darwin's other ideas: he hates slavery and says so, he thinks drinking liquor unhealthy, he believes in the causes of the American and French revolutionaries, and he encourages women's education. As for his personal life: He has twelve children by two wives—he remarries after his first wife dies—and he has three other children who are termed "natural," which means they are not born to either of his wives. He raises two of them as siblings of the other twelve.

Later, his grandson will write about Erasmus:

An etching of an antislavery medallion produced by Josiah Wedgwood in 1787, from The Poetical Works of Erasmus Darwin

He was much in advance of his age in his ideas as to sanitary arrangements—such as supplying towns with pure water, having holes made into crowded sitting and bed-rooms for the constant admission of fresh air, and not allowing chimneys to be closed during summer.

But it is the evolution concept that seems to fascinate Erasmus Darwin most. Just how does change happen in the natural world? Why don't brothers all look exactly alike? Is there a mechanism that creates life's similarities and its differences? How do you explain what are clearly family traits? The Lunaticks can't answer those questions. Erasmus has a grandson who will try. ∎

Annedouche. sc.

Lamarck and Cuvier: Think Oil and Water

What nature does in the course of long periods we do every day when we suddenly change the environment in which some species of living plant is situated.

—Jean-Baptiste Lamarck

Linnaeus and Cuvier have been my two gods, though in very different ways, but they were mere school-boys to old Aristotle.

—Charles Darwin

An illustration of a giraffe from Dictionnaire universel d'histoire naturelle by Charles Dessalines d'Orbigny

When French professor Jean-Baptiste Lamarck (1744–1829) says in the early 1800s that the simplest life-forms gave rise to all others, a few people pay attention, although hardly any agree with him. Lamarck's statement contradicts what is taught in most French schools and goes too far for most people. Is he including us humans? Is he serious?

He is.

Almost everyone still accepts the Great Chain idea, also known as the "fixity of species," which claims that all living forms are exactly as they were when they first appeared on Earth and there have been no major changes to life since the creation. To question that biblical idea, as both Lamarck and Erasmus Darwin do, means swimming against a mainstream current. Actually, more than a current: a riptide.

A portrait of Jean-Baptiste Lamarck, painted in the early 1800s

Lamarck is the eleventh child in a family with upper-class pedigrees but no money. Like many aristocrats of his day, he carries a backpack of names. He is Jean-Baptiste Pierre Antoine de Monet, chevalier de Lamarck.

His brothers have all gone into the army; it is a respectable career for poor nobility. Lamarck's father has different plans for his youngest son. He intends that he be a priest, so he sends him to a Jesuit college.

But Jean-Baptiste, at seventeen, envious of his soldier brothers and following the death of his father, gets on a horse and trots across northern France into Germany, where he joins the French Army. France is fighting a war against Prussia, and volunteers are welcomed. When Lamarck's company is attacked, all the officers are killed. Since he's there and eager, he gets a battlefield promotion. A comrade, meaning to congratulate him, lifts him up by his head, which does enough damage to some of the glands in his neck that he has to leave the army to get treatment in Paris.

From there he is sent to the Mediterranean resort of Monaco to recover. He is given a book on botany to read—and that book sparks a lifelong interest.

But jobs in botany are scarce. Lamarck tries banking, and then medical school, but botany remains a passion. When he visits the Jardin des Plantes in Paris, he is captivated and secures a job there, where he will spend the next ten years working. Salaries are low at the Jardin des Plantes, so Lamarck takes a side job as tutor to the son of Comte de Buffon. Buffon, now quite old, soon becomes his mentor. When Lamarck writes a book about French flowers called *Flore française* (1778), Buffon helps it win popular acclaim, and Lamarck is soon part of France's scientific elite.

In 1789, the bloody French Revolution begins, the monarchy is abolished by a revolutionary government, and King Louis XVI and his queen, Marie Antoinette, are sent to the guillotine, a new French invention that speedily removes a person's head. With all things royal in disfavor, the Jardin des Plantes is reorganized and becomes part of the

A 1793 etching of the execution of the French king Louis XVI

Something Rotten

Although many scientists of her era are trying to understand life, what fascinates Geneviève Thiroux d'Arconville (1720–1805) is nature's process of rotting and decay, which is known as putrefaction.

Though Thiroux d'Arconville's husband serves as a president of the parliament of Paris, she is far more interested in scientific scholarship than politics. She studies English and Italian and becomes fluent enough to translate books into French. She takes science courses at the Jardin des Plantes, in Paris, which holds lectures and exhibitions of scientific research. A woman of wealth, she hosts idea-filled gatherings, sponsors grand balls, finances medical research, and supports a hospice.

But at twenty-two, she catches smallpox and her life changes. When she recovers, she is left with so many facial scars that she no longer wants to throw big parties or even be seen in public. She devotes herself fully to research.

Understanding how to preserve food is vital, since Thiroux d'Arconville lives in a time long before refrigerators, and storing food in cans is still in the future as well. Her interest is sparked when she translates a book by a British doctor who discusses putrefaction, which takes place more quickly in meats and fish if they are not kept cold or preserved by being cured with salt or by some other method.

She builds her own lab and carefully studies how different tissues decay, and even displays some of her ongoing experiments in glass cases she keeps on her mantel. Her 1766 book, *Essay on the History of Putrefaction*, which details hundreds of experiments, is considered a pioneering work in the emerging field. She calls putrefaction "the marvelous operation that nature executes on all organized bodies."

But she works in anonymity, quietly pursuing a scientific career in an era when women are looked down on for doing so, and she leaves her name off her work. Thiroux d'Arconville is part of the wealthy elite whose lives are overturned by the French Revolution. One of her sons is arrested and killed. She is imprisoned. She dies in 1805, after she is allowed to return home.

The title page of a rotten book (actually, a book about rotting)

National Museum of Natural History. Lamarck plays a key role in the new museum, where he is named a professor and curator. He becomes a pioneer in an emerging world of popular science. He classifies invertebrates, writes about the Earth, and becomes an admired lecturer and, soon, a public figure.

As he writes more about geology, it seems clear to him that Earth is very old. What about life? Has it changed over time? That's a big unanswered question. If life has changed, what caused those changes?

In a volume titled *Research on the Organization of Living Bodies*, Lamarck focuses on change in nature. He suggests that change happens when an individual—plant or animal—adjusts to its environment, in a process he calls "transmutation." He says those adjustments can be passed on to progeny. He uses the giraffe as an example. Long-necked giraffes, he says, have evolved from animals that must have stretched their necks to reach food on high branches. Lamarck believes that a lifetime of neck stretching leads to a longer neck and that this trait can be inherited. Lamarck isn't the first to come up with this misguided concept—Erasmus Darwin considered the same idea. In fact, even some of the ancient Greeks did, notably the philosopher Anaximander in the sixth century BCE, who believed humans evolved from other animals.

But Lamarck goes further. In 1800, he explains his evolutionary theory in a paper he reads aloud at Paris's National Museum of Natural History. Modern species, he says, have all descended from a common ancestor over an immense period of time.

He goes on to say that new forms of life are constantly being created by nature itself. How? Lamarck says there must be an innate life fluid, or force, that causes species, given time, to head up a ladder of complexity. He comes up with the idea that the "use and disuse" of body parts can make for changes that can be inherited. Lamarck also says forces in the environment can cause species to change.

Lamarck's big thoughts (and his very big books) appear just as Europe's political winds are reversing themselves. After the openness of the Enlightenment era, the political pendulum is swinging toward a rigid conservatism.

An Ancient View of Evolution

Anaximander believes that humans come from the ocean and that the first people were born, almost fully grown, from sea creatures. This is not true, but it is a bold hypothesis from an ancient Greek philosopher who lives, in what is today Turkey, from 610 to 546 BCE. In a long poem, "On Nature," he says that Earth was once covered with water and that plants and animals came out of the mud. Studying life from land and sea, Anaximander concludes that life-forms change over time.

That's an idea, today known as evolution, that is basic to life science. We're not sure how Anaximander comes to that conclusion, even if it is mixed with many misconceptions, and it will be more than two thousand years before scientists offer evidence to back up such ideas. Today most scientists agree that all life does comes from the ocean, just not in the way Anaximander describes. (A few scientists believe life arrived on Earth from somewhere else, such as Mars or a comet.)

A mosaic image of the ancient Greek philosopher Anaximander, shown holding a sundial

The French Revolution has much to do with it. That revolution leads to a killing spree; it is a warning to some that liberal democracy, without restraints, can go haywire. Besides, thanks in part to France's meddling, Britain has lost thirteen colonies. So the British don't want French ideas—political or scientific—blowing across the channel. At the same time, the German states, humiliated by Napoleon's armies, are refashioning their outlook.

In England, Lamarck's books provoke serious anger; Erasmus Darwin's ideas are attacked too.

To make things worse for Lamarck, he has a powerful enemy at home in France: fossil expert and baron Georges Cuvier (pronounced KOO-vee-ay) (1769–1832). Cuvier rejects the idea of gradual transmutation and then does everything he can to belittle Lamarck.

Cuvier believes that Earth was once home to species that no longer exist. He is the first important scientist to announce that extinctions happen. Studying fossils as no one before him has, Cuvier tries to make sense of what seems to be conflicting evidence. To do so, he divides animal life into four groups and doesn't make one superior to another. He says all are adapted to their habitats. Instead of classifying animals by the way they look on the outside, Cuvier studies their anatomy. For example, he figures out that elephants and fish may not look alike, but both have backbones and are vertebrates. So they are related.

French naturalist Georges Cuvier

In 1796, when he is twenty-seven years old, Cuvier studies the jawbone of a large fossilized *Palaeotherium* (a horse ancestor), which doesn't seem to exist anywhere on Earth. Cuvier writes, "How was it overlooked that it is to fossils alone that must be

France Loses Its Head

Not all French scientists fare as well as Lamarck during the revolution.

Antoine Lavoisier (1743–1794), a famous French chemist mentioned earlier, is credited with an important discovery—that chemical reactions do not lead to either the destruction or creation of matter. For instance, when a fire consumes a building, the matter does not disappear; it is transformed into carbon dioxide and ash and cinders. This concept goes back at least as far as the ancient Greek philosopher Anaxagoras in the fifth century BCE—but Lavoisier does the experimental work to back it up and make it a scientific bedrock.

A scientific couple: Antoine Lavoisier and his wife, Marie Anne

Lavoisier also plays a major role, along with Joseph Priestley, in our understanding of the element oxygen, which he discovers plays a vital role in combustion. He even gives oxygen its name.

But he is unlucky in politics. Before the revolution, he is a member of the prestigious Academy of Sciences in Paris and rejects the work of a young scientist named Jean-Paul Marat, who believes that humans and animals possess an invisible magnetic force that can be harnessed, a theory that does not stand up to scrutiny.

During the revolution, Marat becomes a leader and fixates on getting revenge on Lavoisier. Though Marat is famously murdered in his bathtub in 1793, by then he has succeeded in discrediting Lavoisier. A few months later, in 1794, Lavoisier, like the king and queen and many others, is sent to the guillotine.

"It took them only an instant to cut off that head," said Lavoisier's friend the mathematician Joseph-Louis Lagrange, "and a hundred years may not produce another like it."

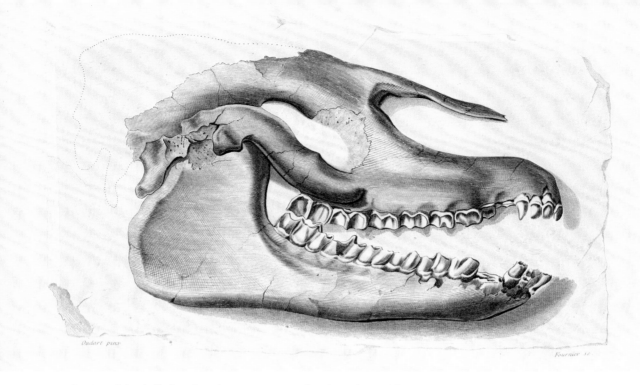

A drawing of the skull of a Palaeotherium, *an extinct four-legged animal first described by Georges Cuvier*

attributed the birth of the theory of the earth; that without them we could never have surmised that there were successive epochs in the formation of the globe?" Of a group of fossils he says, "I only say that they did not originally inhabit the places where we find them at present, and that they must have come from some other part of the globe."

Cuvier finds that changes in fossils often appear where there are abrupt changes in Earth's layers, like those brought on by earthquakes or other catastrophes. So he doesn't see life change as a gradual process. He believes that catastrophes are often followed by rapid changes in life-forms.

Lamarck can't accept Cuvier's catastrophe-based theories. Cuvier can't deal with Lamarck's ideas on gradualism. The intellectual world lines up behind them in two camps known as "uniformitarianism" and "catastrophism."

But it is Cuvier, who is twenty-five years younger than Lamarck, who becomes the celebrity scientist. He soon eclipses Lamarck, who dies poor.

A Sculptor Looks Inside the Body

Dissections of the body and of body parts have been part of medical training in Europe since the time of Andreas Vesalius, an anatomist from the 1500s; by the eighteenth century, anatomical dissections and accompanying lectures are well-attended, popular events. In Paris, both men and women who want to educate themselves in the science of life can watch dissections that were previously intended only for doctors. The dissections draw enthusiastic audiences; some are even held at the Jardin des Plantes.

Marie Marguerite Bihéron (1719–1795), a sculptor who is also a student of anatomy, watches a number of dissections and becomes aware of a problem the medical profession faces: finding dead bodies is difficult, and keeping those bodies from rotting and smelling is often impossible. A friend suggests to Bihéron that she use her skills as a sculptor to cast life models directly from bodies, models that are exact and that doctors and teachers and artists can use for demonstrations and teaching.

So that is what she does. She makes wax models of the body and its internal organs. One newspaper of the day calls them an "anatomical marvel." She uses a wax that doesn't melt (she keeps her wax formula a secret), and she labels body parts in scholarly Latin and Greek.

Bihéron would like to teach, so she moves to England, where there are fewer restrictions on women teaching. She also displays and sells her models of bodies and their parts and internal organs. One of her models is of a pregnant woman, with a fetus that can be removed from the womb.

An eighteenth-century anatomical model with removable organs

Bihéron's work, which is exact and detailed, attracts attention and praise. The Parisian surgeon Sauveur-François Morand becomes a fan, Benjamin Franklin mentions her work in a letter, and the king of Denmark and Empress Catherine the Great of Russia buy her models. Perhaps more important is the commission she receives to make and demonstrate an anatomical model at the Paris Academy of Science.

An advertisement for her demonstrations and lectures explains that, avoiding the "disagreeable circumstances attending the examination of a real corpse . . . the Public may now in the most agreeable manner see how curiously and wonderfully we are made." In other words, there are no smells of decay with her lifelike models and their body parts.

Today we know that Lamarck was often right. His belief that life-forms change over time and his emphasis on the importance of the environment in shaping species were correct. But he was wrong about some things—like the existence of a life fluid and the idea of "use and disuse." Later, his ideas will become known as "soft inheritance," or Lamarckism.

We now know that heredity doesn't work via transmutation. If you are naturally skinny and work hard and develop muscles, it's the skinny build that your offspring will inherit, not the muscles. Throughout much of the twentieth century, Lamarckism is held in low esteem. To be called a Lamarckian means being out of touch or, even worse, accepting nonscientific ideas. But today Lamarck is thought of differently. A twenty-first-century science, epigenetics, that studies the way our genes can turn on or off depending on our environment, has made some of Lamarck's ideas seem ahead of their time. ■

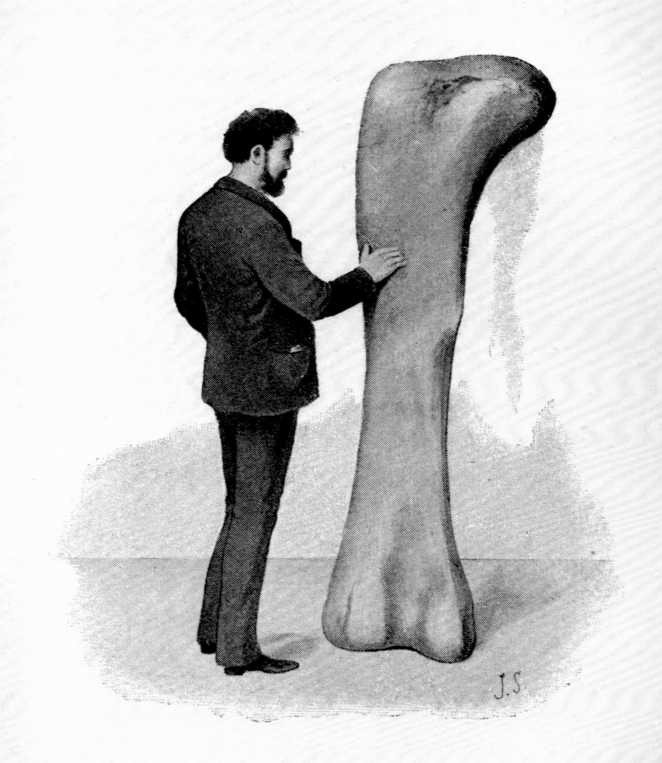

Watch Out for Giants

In the nineteenth century, it was widely believed that animals did not become extinct; any unusual curiosities were explained away as being from animals living undetected in a far-off region of the world.

—Shelley Emling

It would not be wonderful to meet a Megalosaurus, forty feet long or so, waddling like an elephantine lizard up Holborn Hill.

—Charles Dickens

In this drawing from the 1893 book Extinct Monsters, a man stands next to the cast of a dinosaur bone, giving a sense of the dinosaur's size.

Mary Anning (1799–1847) is twelve years old when, in 1811, her brother Joseph finds an unusually large skull in a cliff. Mary becomes fascinated by the skull and spends months searching for and finding much of the rest of the skeleton. But it is not just any skeleton. It belongs to a giant sea creature, long extinct, that could grow to up to 85 feet (26 meters) in length. Eventually, it will be known as an *Ichthyosaurus*, but at the time little is known about it.

Mary's family lives on the chalky coast of Lyme Regis, a town in England with a rocky beach where the locals find fossils to sell to tourists. It is only a few years since Cuvier dug up the *Palaeotherium* bone, and interest in fossils is growing in England. Mary's father, Richard Anning, makes a habit of collecting old bones left uncovered in the sand when the tide rolls out. When Richard is not working as a carpenter and cabinet-maker, he strolls along the beach with Mary, looking for specimens.

Then Richard Anning dies, leaving his family without a source of income. Mary keeps walking the beach, collecting whatever turns up; sometimes she sells what she finds. She has a keen eye and the intellect to go with it. Though she has little formal education, she is soon a self-taught expert on the different kinds of fossils she finds. Lady Harriet Silvester, the widow of a London official, meets Anning in 1824 and records the event in her diary, writing that Mary is:

> so thoroughly acquainted with the science that the moment she finds any bones she knows to what tribe they belong. She fixes the bones on a frame with cement and then makes drawings and has them engraved. . . . It is certainly a wonderful instance of divine favour—that this poor, ignorant girl should be so blessed, for by reading and application she has arrived to that degree of knowledge as to be in the habit of writing and talking with professors and other clever men on the subject, and they all acknowledge that she understands more of the science than anyone else in this kingdom.

A portrait of Mary Anning, fossil hunter

"Poor ignorant girl"? Anning was poor but brilliant, and certainly not ignorant. Lady Harriet, who has some of the class snobbery of her time, doesn't fully understand the depth of Anning's contributions to science. Collectors from London's Geological Society begin turning to her, both for the fossils she finds and for her growing knowledge. She opens her own store, Anning's Fossil Depot. She will be the inspiration for the tongue twister "She sells sea shells on the seashore."

Anning's amazing 1811 discovery of the *Ichthyosaurus* skeleton is the first recognized specimen of its kind. In 1823, Mary Anning finds the first nearly complete example of a *Plesiosaurus*, another sea creature, whose name means "near to reptile." Its neck has thirty-five vertebrae (humans' necks have just seven), and it has two pairs of paddle-like flippers. Among Anning's finds are also *Pterodactylus macronyx*, a flying reptile; and *Squaloraja*, a transitional link between sharks and rays.

Other members of the Anning family participate in the beach digs, but it is Mary who is a scholar by nature and who teaches herself to be a world expert on these ancient creatures. No scientists seem to be studying them as she does. Her specimens, many of which she sells to scholars and private collectors, soon bring needed income to her family. In recognition of her discoveries, members of the British Association for the Advancement of Science and the Geological Society of London eventually set up a fund to compensate her for her work.

Mary Anning's shop, called the Fossil Depot, in the town of Lyme Regis, where she sold her finds

When other fossil hunters hear of Anning's finds, they make their way to Lyme Regis to see what they can dig up. Searching for fossils becomes a popular pursuit in town, which is part of a seaside stretch that comes to be known as the Jurassic Coast.

In 1822, in another part of England called Sussex, a paleontologist couple, Dr. Gideon Mantell (1790–1852) and Mary Ann Mantell (1795–1869), are hunting for fossils in the countryside when they come upon a big tooth. They realize right away that they have something unusual. The tooth, which resembles a lizard's, is clearly very old. Most lizards are tiny creatures; this tooth is more than big—it is gigantic.

Gideon Mantell, a medical doctor, is also an accomplished geologist. He and Mary Ann have been fascinated by some ancient bones recently uncovered in England—like Anning's *Ichthyosaurus*. The Mantells are among those trying to figure out the age of the bones and what kind of creatures they supported, which isn't easy because at this point, no one has discovered a whole skeleton of any of these ancient behemoths. As for the creature that once chewed using the tooth the Mantells find, Gideon names it *Iguanodon* because the peg-like tooth resembles those of a modern iguana.

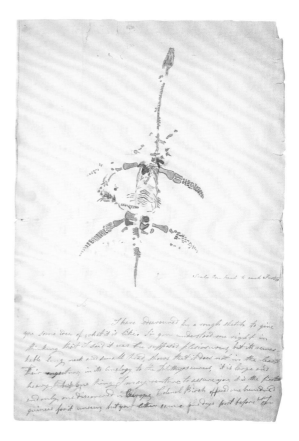

An illustrated letter from Mary Anning about her discovery of a Plesiosaurus skeleton

When Anning dies in 1847, her obituary is read aloud by the president of the Geological Society of London at one of its annual meetings, even though the Geological Society won't admit female members until 1904.

Gideon Mantell, doctor and fossil hunter

Mantell's depiction of an Iguanodon *skeleton*

The Mantells keep digging and discover the front half of a creature they name *Hylaeosaurus* (forest lizard). Then some quarry workers find bones from an ancient skeleton and bring them to Dr. Mantell's door. They are more *Iguanodon* bones.

What exactly are all these bones that are being dug up? Many are unlike any creatures still walking the earth. The Mantells contact the British Museum, and a paleontologist named Sir Richard Owen comes running. Owen realizes the *Iguanodon* fossils are not the bones of a lizard. This animal, whatever it was, had ribs like a crocodile's, hollow limbs like a land animal's (with space for blood vessels and nerves), sharp claws like those of some birds, lower vertebrae attached to the pelvis like a mammal's, toe bones similar to those of a rhinoceros or an elephant, shoulder bones like those of lizards, and size and sculpturing unlike any living animal. They seem to have fallen right out of a child's book of monsters, but clearly these enormous bones were once inside real creatures.

By 1841, the British Association for the Advancement of Science holds a meeting to talk about such fossils. At the meeting, Richard Owen names fossils of this kind "dinosauria," from Greek words meaning "terrible reptiles."

Soon the word *dinosaur* is in popular use, giving the strange bones an identity. Now that fossil hunters have something with a name to look for, public attention increases and bones begin turning up everywhere. Imagine the excitement each time someone finds another bone from one of these marvelous creatures. How do the bones fit together? What did the "terrible reptiles" actually look like?

This is all new, and it captures the popular imagination. Within a few years, Queen Victoria herself will be opening a giant exhibition featuring a dinosaur replica.

By the early 1850s, Owen is working with a sculptor, Benjamin Waterhouse Hawkins, who is making a huge iron, brick, and concrete replica of an *Iguanodon*. London has just held one of the big cultural events of the century: an 1851 exhibition of science and

Mantell's illustration imagining what an Iguanodon *might have looked like*

technology staged in a new glass-and-steel building dubbed the Crystal Palace. People from all over the world came to see the wonders displayed in the palace. Queen Victoria opened the event herself.

It's all so popular that after the exhibition closes, the decision is made to rebuild and expand the Crystal Palace, moving it to Sydenham, south of London. Hawkins

An etching of Sir Richard Owen with the skeleton of a large extinct bird

Sculptor Benjamin Waterhouse Hawkins

builds a series of the first giant dinosaur replicas for the new site. Invitations to the 1853 opening are sent to twenty-one eminent naturalists. Those invitations are printed on a replica of the wing bone of a pterodactyl, a species Anning discovered. Celebrity scientists are treated to a seven-course dinner inside the *Iguanodon*'s belly. The dinosaur's back is removed, a

The Iguanodon *dinner party*

Take a Breath

Modern paleontologist Peter Ward argues that the amount of oxygen in the atmosphere changed dramatically (both increasing and decreasing) during the time of dinosaurs but that they avoided extinctions that affected other species. Why? Perhaps because their air sacs (a unique breathing system inherited by modern birds) helped in oxygen-depleted times.

Although insects and mammals adapted to the arrival of flowering plants, taking advantage of this new potential food source, dinosaurs did not. Most couldn't climb trees. But some avian dinosaurs—birds—were an exception. While many birds in this era, known as the Cretaceous Period, had teeth, others developed beaks, which enabled them to forage for a wider variety of food. That would prove to be a critical advantage. Scientists believe a giant asteroid that landed in the Gulf of Mexico sixty-six million years ago created an immense dust cloud that blotted out the sun and led to the extinction of many of Earth's inhabitants, including most dinosaurs. Beaked birds were an exception, since they can dig into the dirt for seeds and nuts, giving them an advantage in this desolate period.

Birds of a Feather

In 1861, some Bavarian stonecutters find a fossil with the teeth, sharp claws, long legs, and bony tail of a reptile but the wings and feathers of a bird. An elegant little fossil, it is about the size of a blue jay; Richard Owen buys it for the British Museum. That 150-million-year-old creature, which seems to fit somewhere between bird and dinosaur, is named *Archaeopteryx*, meaning "ancient feather."

We now know that some dinosaurs were feathered while others had skin of tough leathery plates. Some had horns; some were duck-billed. Some could fly; perhaps all could swim. Some ate meat; some were vegetarian. Some were bipeds, meaning they walked on two feet, and some were quadrupeds, meaning they walked on four feet. Dinosaurs evolved into more than a thousand different varieties. Many had active social networks. All stood erect, in contrast to reptiles that crawl. That erect stance gave them speed and helped with breathing too. Recent research suggests that female dinosaurs were often pregnant by age eight and that many died by about thirty.

A drawing of archaeopteryxes from a 1928 book about evolution

Whether birds are direct descendants of dinosaurs or cousins, as some experts believe, they have done very well for themselves in the centuries after the dinosaurs. There are "9,000 living species of birds, compared with 4,100 species of mammals," says John Noble Wilford, author of *The Riddle of the Dinosaur*. As for dinosaurs, if you picture them as pea-brained misfits, erase that thought. They ruled Earth from the late Triassic period (230 million years ago) to the Cretaceous (65 million years ago), a span of about 165 million years, which is much longer than human history.

striped tent is raised above the iron beast, and a dinner table is set with china, silver, and candles. The guests sing a song that includes these words:

The jolly old beast
Is not deceased.
There's life in him again.

Hawkins soon travels to the United States, where he is hired to build dinosaur replicas for a grand new Paleozoic Museum that is to be built in New York City's Central Park. He works for three years on the soaring replicas. But unfortunately, he runs afoul of New York politics at a time when the city's political machine is particularly corrupt. William Tweed, known as "Boss" Tweed, is a New York State senator who controls much of the city, and he decides to abandon the museum. After Hawkins publicly protests the decision, Tweed's men break into his workshop and destroy his replicas, whose remains are buried in a pit and have never been found.

But Hawkins's work is not entirely absent in America. He creates a life-size mounted skeleton of a giant hadrosaur, using real bones with artificial ones to fill in gaps, and gives it as a gift to the Academy of Natural Sciences in Philadelphia. It is not entirely accurate, but the towering creature is a hit, bringing a dinosaur exhibit to America for the first time. It is so popular that the academy's leadership is concerned by the overwhelming response.

Benjamin Waterhouse Hawkins with his hadrosaur skeleton

"The crowds lead to many accidents, the sum total of which amounts to a considerable destruction of property, in the way of broken glass, light wood work, etc.," they write in a report following the dinosaur exhibit. "Further, the excessive clouds of dust produced by the moving crowds, rest upon the horizontal cases, obscuring from view their contents, while it penetrates others much to the detriment of parts of the collection."

Long extinct, dinosaurs are back. ∎

Erasmus's Grandson

A fool . . . is a man who never tried an experiment in his life.

—Erasmus Darwin

I love fools' experiments. I am always making them.

—Charles Darwin

Young Charles Darwin with his sister Catherine

A painting of Charles Darwin (1809–1882), age seven, shows him holding a potted plant. It seems a curious choice for a little boy, but Darwin, writing his autobiography many years later, says, "I was interested at this early age in the variability of plants!" He even confesses to a childish fib based on this early fascination: he told one of his playmates that he could produce colored primroses by watering them with colored water, which sounds plausible. Later, he recalls it as "a monstrous fable."

When Charles is eight, his mother, Susannah Wedgwood Darwin, dies. Three older sisters will help raise him. A few months after his mother's death, he begins attending a nearby day school. "I have been told that I was much slower in learning than my younger sister Catherine," he would later write, "and I believe that I was in many ways a naughty boy."

At age nine, Charles joins his brother, Erasmus (known as Raz), at the Shrewsbury School, a prestigious boarding school a mile from their home. The schoolmaster is not impressed with young Charles. Later, Darwin says, "Nothing could have been worse for the development of my mind than Dr. Butler's school, as it was strictly classical," noting that "especial attention was paid to verse-making, and this I could never do well." Further, Darwin comments:

The Shrewsbury School, where young Charles Darwin was a student

> I was considered by all my masters and by my father as a very ordinary boy, rather below the common standard in intellect. To my deep mortification my father once said to me, "You care for nothing but shooting, dogs, and rat-catching, and you will be a disgrace to yourself and all your family."

That isn't quite fair of his father to say; Darwin is learning, but in his own way. Later, he remembers studying Euclid, and "the intense satisfaction which the clear geometrical proofs gave me." As for reading, he "used to sit for hours reading the historical plays of Shakespeare, generally in an old window in the thick walls of the school."

He doesn't get good grades, and today he might have had trouble getting into college, but Darwin's influential father has no problem enrolling him, at age sixteen, at the University of Edinburgh, where Raz is studying medicine. It is the career their doctor father intends for them both. Five years apart, the two boys have spent hours together in a backyard chemistry lab stocked with their grandfather Josiah Wedgwood's made-to-their-order equipment. Writing of Raz, Charles says, "I was allowed to aid him as a servant in most of his experiments. He made all the gases and many compounds, and I read with care several books on chemistry."

An 1829 engraving of the University of Edinburgh

Darwin likes to assemble things. "I tried to make out the names of plants, and collected all sorts of things, shells, seals, franks, coins, and minerals. The passion for collecting . . . was very strong in me, and was clearly innate, as none of my sisters or brother ever had this taste." In Edinburgh, he goes right on collecting, identifying, organizing, and making notes on what for him are treasures. At the same time, he does a lot of reading about plants and animals. From 1825 to 1826, Charles and Raz check out more books from the university library than any

Josiah Wedgwood, Erasmus Darwin's Lunatick friend, was not only Charles Darwin's grandfather; he was also the grandfather of Emma Wedgwood, who became Charles's wife. Charles and Emma were first cousins. Today we know that when firsts cousins marry, their children may inherit health and reproductive problems. This may be why, of Charles and Emma's ten children, three die in childhood.

other borrowers. Charles's checkout list includes Newton's *Optics* (1704), Boswell's *Life of Johnson* (1791), and William Wood's *Illustrations of the Linnean Genera of Insects* (1821), along with a fair number of medical books.

In addition, these wealthy young brothers buy well-regarded books, and they also have access to a local lending library. They go to lectures, to concerts, to churches (so they can compare sermons); they also hike and explore. Charles keeps notes on the birds, bugs, fish, and shells he finds. He is training himself to be a naturalist and a scholar, but he also reads works of fiction. ("I have been most shockingly idle, actually reading two novels at once," he writes to his sister.) On April 26, 1826, in a stagecoach heading home, he makes note of the first chimney swallows of the season. He is compulsive about recording whatever he sees.

The next year, when Charles comes back to Edinburgh, it is without Raz, who is studying medicine in London. Charles studies natural science with Robert Jameson, who is Edinburgh's leading geologist. Jameson is working on a translation of Georges Cuvier's works from French into English. Most British scholars agree with Cuvier's rejection of the transmutation idea and his belief that each species was created

Charles Darwin's brother, Erasmus, will get his medical degree, become a London socialite, and eventually, like the fictional Sherlock Holmes, become addicted to opium. He will never practice medicine.

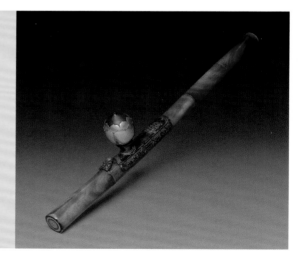

A nineteenth-century opium pipe

to perfectly fit its environment and therefore remains unchanged unless it goes extinct. Professor Robert Jameson agrees too. And so does young Darwin.

But Darwin finds Professor Jameson's lectures "incredibly dull," and after doing some of his classroom assignments, he makes a promise (which he won't keep) never to read another geology book. Meanwhile, Darwin is finding Edinburgh a congenial place. He joins a scientific club called the Plinian Society and pursues his obsession with cataloging and classifying. The city is perched on an ancient volcano, making it a kind of real-life geological textbook. Darwin can see Earth's layers in the land around the city and begins to understand that Earth must be very old.

A portrait of the geologist Robert Jameson

Studying on his own with John Edmonstone, a local taxidermist, Darwin learns to stuff and mount birds. Edmonstone works with a local museum in Edinburgh. Years earlier, he was enslaved on a plantation in Guyana, north of Brazil in South America. Like those of many other enslaved people, his last name came from the owner of the plantation, a Scotsman named Charles Edmonstone.

The naturalist Charles Waterton, a friend of Charles Edmonstone, visited that Guyana plantation in the early 1800s (in 1825, he will publish a popular book about his travels). Waterton is an unusual personality, known for talking to insects and sometimes barking like a dog at dinner parties. He took John Edmonstone, then held in bondage, with him on his travels in the Guyanese jungle and taught him taxidermy, or, as Waterton puts it, "the proper way to do birds."

John Edmonstone went on to become an expert in the field. By 1817, he has joined Charles Edmonstone in Scotland, where slavery has been banned. John, now free, will work at museums in Glasgow and Edinburgh, earning a living stuffing birds and teaching taxidermy.

John Edmondstone and Charles Darwin

Charles Darwin, at age sixteen, becomes one of his students. Darwin is captivated by Edmonstone's descriptions of the rich flora and fauna of South America. "He gave me lessons for payment, and I used often to sit with him, for he was a very pleasant and intelligent man," Darwin writes, and also says that he "spent many hours in conversation at his side." Edmonstone may have planted seeds in Darwin's head that would later make him eager to visit South America, though his name is never mentioned by Darwin and is only uncovered later by those studying Darwin's life.

In Edinburgh, another friend, Robert Grant, teaches Darwin to use a microscope as a scientific tool. Grant is a fan of both Lamarck and Erasmus Darwin. At a meeting of the Plinian Society, Charles Darwin reads a paper he has written describing his microscopic examination of larvae. Together, Grant and Darwin dissect tiny marine creatures they have collected in the Firth of Forth, an estuary flowing into the North Sea from Edinburgh.

Although he doesn't talk about it, being the grandson of a famous man gives Darwin status at the university. He says he wants to be just another student, but that's impossible. Everyone knows Erasmus Darwin's writings, especially his key scientific work, *Zoonomia*, which includes his ideas about transmutation. Charles Darwin says that when he first read the work, it didn't produce "any effect on me," and he will later say he is disappointed by what he sees as its overreliance on speculation, but he also says that its ideas probably helped form the basis of his notions about evolution.

As for studying medicine, it never becomes a passion for Charles. Medical training is not as it had been a century earlier, when university courses gave aspiring doctors little practical training. In Darwin's time, it is mandatory for would-be doctors to observe operations. Those operations are performed without anesthesia and with no understanding that cleanliness can help prevent the spread of disease. Later, writing about his experience as a medical student, Darwin says, "I . . . saw two very bad operations, one on a child, but I rushed away before they were completed. Nor did I ever attend again, for hardly any inducement would have been strong enough to make me do so. . . . The two cases fairly haunted me for many a long year."

Darwin can be a doctor without being a surgeon, so that's not his problem; he just doesn't want to become a doctor, at least not enough to work at it. By the end of his second year in Edinburgh, he has made up his mind: he is not going to be a doctor. What will become of him? His father, fearing he will be a failure in life, sends him off to Cambridge University; with a Cambridge degree he can become a Church of England minister. That is an acceptable career for a nineteenth-century English gentleman. Darwin isn't enthusiastic about it, but he doesn't have any other goal, and he is a devout Christian. "I did not then in the least doubt the strict and literal truth of every word in the Bible," he will write later in his autobiography. At Cambridge, his faith is solidified when he studies natural theology with the well-respected William Paley. Paley expresses no doubt about the active role of God in creating the wonders of nature.

Christ's College, part of Cambridge University, in an 1838 etching

Meanwhile, Darwin is still cataloging everything that intrigues him.

No pursuit at Cambridge was followed with nearly so much eagerness or gave me so much pleasure as collecting beetles. . . . One day, on tearing off some old bark, I saw two

rare beetles, and seized one in each hand; then I saw a third and new kind, which I could not bear to lose, so that I popped the one which I held in my right hand into my mouth. Alas! It ejected some intensely acrid fluid, which burnt my tongue so that I was forced to spit the beetle out, which was lost.

Darwin is collecting and classifying well enough to impress some Cambridge experts. One of his beetles turns up in a book on British insects. He is thrilled to get this credit: "captured by C. Darwin, Esq."

While Darwin is at Cambridge, John Stevens Henslow's botany lectures are the talk of the local community. An academic superstar, Henslow is training a generation of

Darwin's beetle box at the Cambridge University Museum of Zoology

botanists to take a hands-on approach, studying plants for themselves in the field and making their own observations of the plants' characteristics. Darwin regularly attends his lectures; Henslow invites him on nature walks and also to his home for family dinners and social evenings. Henslow likes the quiet young man who is serious about observing, collecting, and cataloging nature, so he arranges for him to go on a field trip to North Wales with geologist Adam Sedgwick. Ever since he studied under the dull Jameson, Darwin has avoided further study in geology, but this excursion makes him think more deeply about the Earth and its layers.

John Stevens Henslow, botanist

Sedgwick, impressed by the work Darwin does on their trip, predicts a brilliant future for him. Darwin has begun to do well in school: he graduates without honors but a respectable tenth in a class of 178, and with his bachelor of arts.

About this time, he reads Alexander von Humboldt's *Personal Narrative* and is enthralled. Humboldt describes wonders: the sky-scratching Andes Mountains; the awesome Amazon River, six miles (9.5 kilometers) wide at one place; and plants and animals so gorgeous that it is not surprising that many believe South America to be the site of the Garden of Eden. Darwin memorizes long passages from Humboldt, then recites them aloud again and again (which is more than some of his friends can handle). Darwin says the book "stirred up in me a burning zeal to add even the most humble contribution to the noble structure of Natural Science."

Adam Sedgwick, geologist

Inspired by Humboldt, Darwin makes plans to visit Tenerife, in the Canary Islands. It is to be a last fling before he settles into life as an Anglican minister. But the trip falls

An 1854 painting of a South American scene by Frederic Edwin Church, who was inspired by the travel writing of Alexander von Humboldt

apart; then an unpaid position turns up on the HMS *Beagle*, a ten-gun brig sloop of the Royal Navy, which is setting out on a research voyage. Professor Henslow has been offered the opening, but he isn't interested; he suggests Darwin in his place.

The ship's captain, aristocratic Robert Fitzroy, also in his twenties, is looking for a naturalist to sail with him, and he must be of the upper class. England is a hierarchical place where a captain can't mingle with sailors, and Fitzroy, a man of high intelligence and strong religious faith, wants someone to talk with during the voyage. To Darwin it sounds like a great adventure. The *Beagle* is a small ship, about 90 feet (27.5 meters)

HMS Beagle *exploring the coast of Tierra del Fuego*

long, with a crew of more than sixty, but it carries the latest equipment. Its mission is to chart the South American coast and also to take measurements of longitude at uncharted spots around the globe. Both tasks will be done well by the talented, efficient, and high-strung Fitzroy.

Darwin's father has reservations about the voyage. He thinks his son is putting off a serious commitment to his future, but his uncle Josiah Wedgwood II (the potter Josiah Wedgwood's son) says it might be the making of the young man. This turns out to be an understatement.

When Charles Darwin climbs aboard the *Beagle*, it is December 1831 and he is twenty-two years old. ■

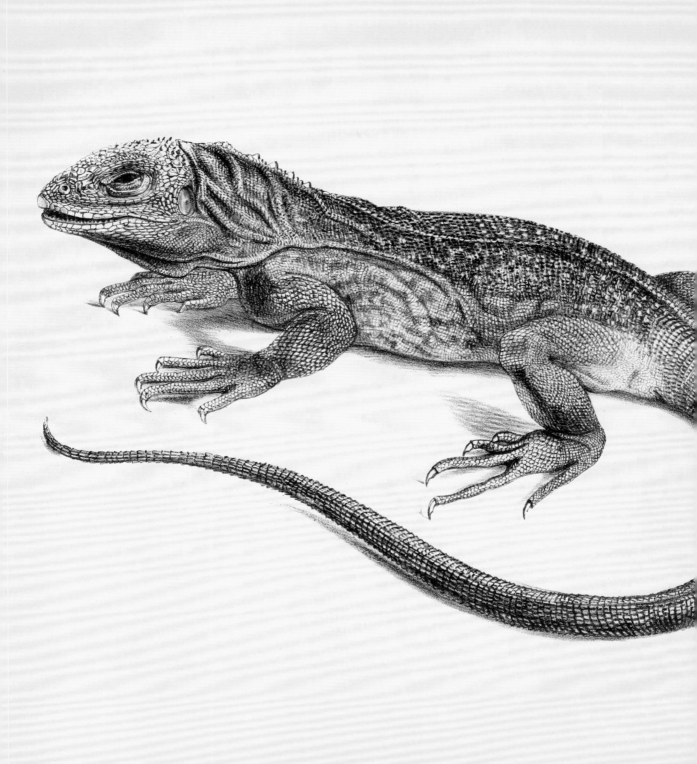

Aboard the *Beagle*: Five Years at Sea

It must have appeared almost as improbable to the earlier geologists, that the laws of earthquakes should one day throw light on the origin of mountains, as it must to the first astronomers, that the fall of an apple should assist in explaining the motions of the moon.

—Charles Lyell

Seeing every height crowned with its crater, and the boundaries of most of the lava-streams still distinct, we are led to believe that within a period geologically recent the unbroken ocean was here spread out. Hence, both in space and time, we seem to be brought somewhat near to that great fact—the mystery of mysteries—the first appearance of new beings on this earth.

—Charles Darwin

An illustration of an iguana from Darwin's five-volume work, The Zoology of the Voyage of H.M.S. *Beagle*

Darwin carries a new book, *Principles of Geology*, with him onto the *Beagle*. Written by geologist Charles Lyell, its central idea is that the present is the key to the past. Lyell theorizes that the Earth was formed over eons by natural forces—such as earthquakes, volcanoes, and erosion—that have changed our planet and continue to do so.

Thanks to Lyell (and some others), Darwin understands that the Earth is ancient and has a long story to tell. He will search for that story in rocks and layers and in the

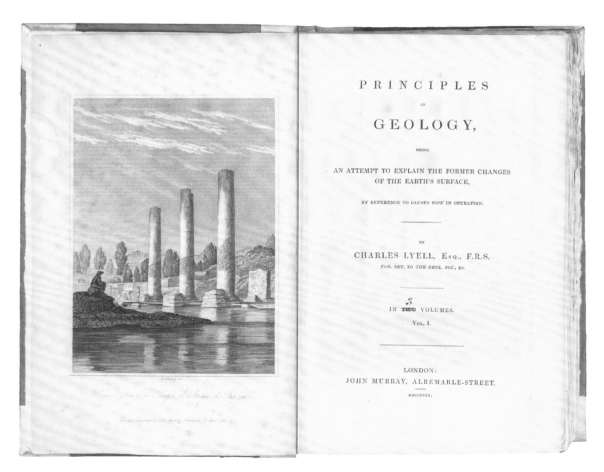

Charles Lyell's Principles of Geology

links he finds between geography, climate, and life-forms. Darwin realizes that the fossils Lyell has documented are different from one another because they come from different rock levels, which each carry a squashed layer of time. Darwin hopes to make his own discoveries; he brings a diary and notebooks so he can carefully document what he finds.

Darwin is reading Lyell's book when the *Beagle* makes its first two stops; both are at Cape Verde, a horseshoe-shaped necklace of small volcanic islands some 350 miles (560 kilometers) off the northwest coast of Africa. There, where mountainous islands carry deep erosion scars, he can see for himself the dramatic power of nature's geological forces.

Lyell and Darwin don't agree with most of their educated peers, who believe that the Earth and its inhabitants were all created about six thousand years ago and have remained mostly unchanged. But when it comes to life-forms, Lyell and Darwin do agree with the scientific and religious thinking of the day, which mistakenly maintains that every organism on Earth—from mushrooms and bugs to trees and humans—is the product of a separate and divine creation, unconnected to others and perfectly adapted to its environment.

Cape Verde's Pico de Fogo, a still-active volcano

Picture Darwin as the *Beagle* approaches Cape Verde: it is January of 1832, and he is standing on the deck of the ship, a proper young English gentleman who wears a topcoat with tails, a buttoned waistcoat, a high-collared shirt, and a cravat (a fancy kind of tie). He is focusing his new binoculars on cliffs of hardened lava. He now thinks that perhaps he may write a book on geology. (He will publish *Geological Observations on the Volcanic Islands* in 1844.)

He has brought on board a carpetbag that holds, among other things, slippers, walking shoes, and twelve shirts. He also has a compass, pistols, a new microscope, a magnifying glass, and jars of spirits for preserving specimens. As for books, in addition to Lyell, he has a Bible, Milton's *Paradise Lost*, and books in Spanish, a language he is attempting to master. A library on board includes 245 volumes; some are about places the ship will visit.

Here he is describing one of his first explorations: "On the shores of Quail Island, I found fragments of brick, bolts of iron, pebbles . . . united . . . into a firm conglomerate." Darwin, who has been collecting and classifying much of his life, is interested in everything he sees, even the dust in the air in mid-ocean. "The dust falls in such quantities as to dirty everything on board, and to hurt people's eyes," he writes. Darwin sends packets of dust to Christian Gottfried Ehrenberg, a leading expert in microscopic life, who will find "no less than sixty-seven different organic forms" in it. Although Professor Ehrenberg "knows many species of *infusoria* [microbes] peculiar to Africa," Darwin will note, "he finds none of these in the dust which I sent him. On the other hand, he finds in it two species which hitherto he knows as living only in South America."

On February 29, 1832, the *Beagle* makes landfall at Salvador, a town in the state of Bahia, Brazil, in northeastern South America. Darwin is ecstatic to be on the South American continent. "Delight," he writes, "is a weak term to express the feelings of a naturalist who, for the first time, has wandered by himself in a Brazilian forest. The elegance of the grasses, the novelty of the parasitical plants, the beauty of the flowers, the glossy green of the foliage, but above all the general luxuriance of the vegetation, filled me with admiration."

All Darwin's senses are at work. "The noise from the insects is so loud, that it may be heard even in a vessel anchored several hundred yards from the shore; yet within the recesses of the forest a universal silence appears to reign. To a person fond of natural history, such a day as this brings with it a deeper pleasure than he can ever hope to experience again."

Dust in the Wind

Exactly what is dust? Scientifically, dust forms when common rock minerals (like silica, calcium carbonite, and iron oxides) are broken down into sand and even smaller particles. Those particles can get blown around the globe. Earth's deserts, like the Gobi and Sahara, are major sources of dust. Desert dust contains iron and, when transported to iron-poor regions of the ocean, may bring vital nutrients to whales and fish.

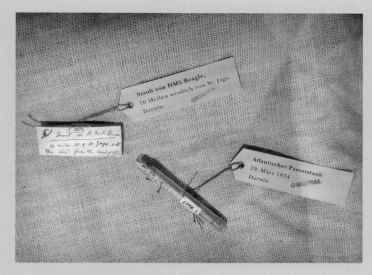

Vials of dust collected by Darwin

Dust particles from deserts can sometimes darken the sky in other nearby and even faraway locations. A 2001 storm blown by winds from Siberia was labeled "the perfect dust storm." It turned day into night and, according to a NASA report, sent "millions of tons of dust from the Gobi and Taklimakan Deserts" to eastern Asia's cities, and from there across the Pacific to North America, where it was a "white haze" in the sky. An ongoing project called the "Great Green Wall" of China, which has led to the cultivation of thousands of miles of forestland near the Gobi Desert, is an effort to control such dust storms.

In Bahia, Darwin encounters his first tropical storm. "I tried to find shelter under a tree, which was so thick that it would never have been penetrated by common English rain; but here, in a couple of minutes, a little torrent flowed down the trunk."

Captain Fitzroy is expected to chart the South American coast. That means the *Beagle* will sail back and forth along that coast for month after month after month. The ship

Perched on a triangular peninsula lapped by bay and ocean, multicultural Bahia was a strategic point of contention in the sixteenth century, battled over by Dutch, Spanish, and Portuguese invaders. Imposing themselves on the native population, some of the European interlopers eventually created sugar plantations using the labor of kidnapped and enslaved people from Africa. Brazilian colonizers will bring over far more enslaved Africans than will be brought to the United States.

An illustration of some toucans that Darwin would have seen on the voyage of the HMS Beagle

carries small open research boats that can be lowered and rowed into coves and, when necessary, pulled easily onto land. While the meticulous Fitzroy is working on his charts, Darwin is free to leave the ship, hire guides (which he has the means to do), and explore. Every few weeks or months, the *Beagle* and its naturalist rendezvous, but mostly he does whatever he wishes. Since he suffers mightily from seasickness, no one urges him to stay on board.

In April, the *Beagle* anchors at the Brazilian city of Rio de Janeiro, and Darwin heads inland for two weeks of exploration (still dressed in proper English attire). The route is through a thick tropical forest, where everything, especially the butterflies, is brilliantly colored. Many of the birds, beasts, and bugs, including lizards and cockroaches, are bigger than anything he has imagined. Howler monkeys provide background noise to the chatter of yellow and red parrots and the loud croaks of rainbow-beaked toucans—and all are part of a jungle symphony that often includes long moments of eerie silence.

Darwin finds anthill cones that are almost 12 feet (3.5 meters) high. Slender cabbage palms, tall as ship's masts, soar toward the sky. Flamboyant orchids spark what will become a lifelong fascination for Darwin. Then, as now, this region is as biologically diverse as any place on Earth.

Darwin writes to his old botany professor Henslow, "I shall have a large box to send very soon to Cambridge." His collections and his notes go to England on British naval ships that call at South American ports. Six months later, after the first box arrives, Professor Henslow responds, "You have done wonders."

Martin Johnson Heade's 1871 painting Cattleya Orchid and Three Hummingbirds. *Heade traveled in South America and was inspired by Darwin's ideas about the relationship of animals to their environments.*

Darwin meets an Irishman who invites him to his Brazilian plantation. He finds it run by enslaved labor. Darwin is horrified, especially after he witnesses a violent incident. In his writings, he describes many other atrocities. "I have seen a boy, six or seven years old, struck thrice with a horse whip (before I could interfere) on his naked head, for having handed me a glass of water not quite clean," he recounts.

Erasmus Darwin was among England's early abolitionists. His grandson can see nothing positive in slavery either. About the slave trade, young Darwin says it makes his "blood boil, yet heart tremble" to know that it still exists and that Englishmen and Americans are still part of it.

This 1830 painting by Benedito Calixto depicts enslaved laborers harvesting and processing sugar cane on a Brazilian plantation.

For Captain Fitzroy, slavery is an orderly system of labor that can be traced to biblical times. Darwin is not typically confrontational, but when they clash on this issue, the two usually friendly men grow angry and argue. For a time it seems like Darwin might be forced off the ship, before Fitzroy apologizes.

Captain Robert Fitzroy

Fitzroy and his crew head back north to Bahia to do more surveying and to set the longitude of Rio de Janeiro, which hasn't been done before and will be used as a measure to chart other places. Darwin stays behind and rents a cottage near Rio, where he lives with the ship's artist, Augustus Earle. Darwin hunts toucans, parrots, and monkeys, dissects the specimens, and conducts experiments, such as studying the regeneration of a worm that had been cut into two parts. Earle paints. Darwin writes to his sister Catherine, "You cannot imagine anything more calmly and delightfully than these weeks."

By July, the *Beagle* turns south, stopping at the great port of Montevideo, in Uruguay. Between stops, Darwin's research continues while he is on the *Beagle*. He lowers a net astern into the ocean and hauls out quantities of small sea creatures, which he spreads on the deck, to the dismay of some of the crew (they are not collectors, and he makes a mess). Alongside the ship, whales and dolphins spout and leap.

As they head south, the weather cools. Darwin trains a crew member, Syms Covington, to be his assistant. Syms learns to skin and stuff birds and other creatures. Eventually he will do much of the shooting and gathering of birds and other specimens for Darwin's collection, and he will continue working for Darwin after the voyage.

The *Beagle* continues on, now heading for high-peaked Tierra del Fuego, an archipelago near the cold tip of South America. Three Indigenous people from Tierra del Fuego are on board the *Beagle*. Four years earlier, Captain Fitzroy kidnapped them in coastal South America and brought them to England. They have been educated in

British ways, baptized, clothed in English apparel, and given new names. (A fourth died of smallpox in London.)

Darwin has open-minded views (for his day). Historians Adrian Desmond and James Moore comment that his time with John Edmonstone "confirmed Darwin's belief that black and white men possessed the same essential humanity." By his own account, the people of Tierra del Fuego are as puzzled by the Europeans as the Europeans are of them.

But he also calls the Indigenous people he encounters "savages" and views himself and his colleagues as a civilizing force. Fitzroy's kidnapping of Indigenous people is viewed in contemporary Western accounts as an act of charity; they are even trotted out for an audience with the king.

A depiction of Fuegians and a visitor from the Beagle *exchanging greetings, from Robert Fitzroy's account of the voyage*

Fitzroy returns the trio to their home on this trip and brings a British missionary too. The captain has high hopes: he expects these four to Christianize the region. The London Missionary Society has sent goods that they feel would be useful to help transform the Fuegians' land; they include tea trays, wineglasses, soup bowls, beaver hats, and chamber pots.

After anchoring the *Beagle*, crew members get into surveying boats and row ashore to look for relatives of the three locals, who are of the Yaghan and Alacaluf peoples. The British crew spends five days unloading supplies; they build three large tents and plant seeds.

The Yaghan relatives of one of the kidnapped people appear, but Darwin says the man's native language skills have grown rusty. He tries to speak to his brother in English, then in Spanish. They look at each other, baffled. Others come into view. Darwin estimates about 120 of them. The sailors need a bonfire to keep warm, but even with it and their heavy clothes, they shiver;

A drawing of an Indigenous Fuegian from Fitzroy's account of the Beagle *voyage*

the Yaghans approach the flames and perspire, according to Darwin's notes.

"They were delighted at our dancing and singing, and were particularly interested at seeing us wash in a neighbouring brook; they did not pay much attention to anything else, not even to our boats." Suddenly, "every woman and child disappeared. We were all uneasy at this." Fitzroy decides that the three newly returned locals, the missionary (Richard Matthews), and the other Indigenous people all need time to adjust to one another. So he and the crew climb into their boats and head off to do some exploring.

Darwin writes of the "mysterious grandeur in mountain behind mountain, with the deep intervening valleys, all covered by one thick, dusky mass of forest." Deep inlets descend into the Straits of Magellan, creating awesome vistas. But it is not pretty scenery that affects Darwin. He writes, "The atmosphere . . . in this climate, where gale succeeds gale, with rain, hail, and sleet, seems blacker than anywhere else." After ten days, the exploring party is ready to head back to the encampment.

Mountains and glaciers in the Strait of Magellan

Things there have not gone as planned. (Would you trust people who had kidnapped your relatives?) The crew find that most of the supplies they brought have disappeared, and the Yaghans are not happy to see the Brits return. They are not afraid of guns, since they have never encountered them before, but they do have weapons of their own.

The *Beagle* crew departs, taking Matthews with them, and heads for the Falkland Islands, off South America's Atlantic coast. Then they return to Montevideo. There, in 1832, Darwin receives the second volume of Lyell's work, in which Lyell uses the word *evolution* in its modern sense of change over time; in the book, Lyell attacks Lamarck's ideas on change, although he does so thoughtfully.

Montevideo is a departure point for Darwin; from there he heads for the broad Argentine pampas, sharing life in the saddle with gauchos (cowboys), while collecting and studying. Darwin is especially fascinated by the birds he tracks; most are new to him. At Punta Alta, in Argentina, on September 23, he finds the jawbone of a gigantic fossilized sloth, which once may have weighed as much as two pickup trucks. This is his first great find. He sends it and some other fossils to England.

In Punta Alta, where vegetation is sparse, he and Syms Covington take pickaxes and hack away at hills of gravel, seashells, and dried mud. They uncover the fossilized remains of *Megatherium*, an extinct sloth that weighed five tons (4.5 metric tons) and stood on two feet; *Toxodon*, which looked like a combination of rhino and hippo; an elephant-like mastodon; a giant armadillo; and horse fossils.

Horse fossils? There were no known horses in the Americas when the first sixteenth-century European invaders arrived; those that the gauchos ride are descended from horses brought from Europe. How can these horse fossils be explained? And what about the giant animal fossils? Darwin sees no giants among the living species around him. The Indigenous people tell him that certain rivers make bones grow, but he thinks otherwise. Darwin believes that these huge fossils are of animals related to smaller animal species now living. But what happened to the giants?

How do big animals survive in a jungle environment? Darwin thinks and thinks about this and concludes that tropical vegetation is not necessary for large animals, and perhaps open savannas may be better for giant plant eaters like elephants.

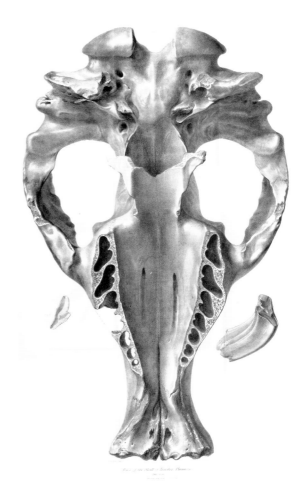

A drawing of a Toxodon *skull from Darwin's* Zoology of the Voyage of H.M.S. *Beagle*

Darwin continues on horseback and notes that the landscape keeps changing. One day he rides to a large and shallow salt lake, which turns into "a field of snow-white salt" in summers. The lake is bordered by black and stinky mud, inhabited in some parts by worms and also containing crystals. "How surprising it is that any creatures should be able to exist in brine, and that they should be crawling among crystals of sulphate of soda and lime," Darwin writes.

Large numbers of flamingos live around the lake and breed there, likely burrowing with their beaks for worms. Darwin is fascinated. "We have a little living world within itself, adapted to these inland lakes of brine," he writes. "Well may we affirm that every part of the world is habitable! Whether lakes of brine, those subterranean ones hidden beneath volcanic mountains—warm mineral springs—the wide expanse and depths of the ocean—the upper regions of the atmosphere, and even the surface of perpetual snow—all support organic beings."

Life in underground pits of brine? In the depths of the ocean? In the upper regions of the atmosphere? Darwin, who has new ideas racing around in his head, is now aware that mountains erode, that rivers change and so do life-forms. Studying a relative of the rattlesnake, he notes "how every character . . . has a tendency to vary by slow degrees."

Darwin packs up skins of two hundred birds and sends them to Henslow, along with preserved fish, bugs, beetles, and rodents, huge fossil bones, and notes. The scientific community in Great Britain is awed.

Then the *Beagle* heads back to check again on the people it returned to Tierra del Fuego, several months after they left. "A canoe, with a little flag flying" appears, Darwin writes. It is carrying one of the men who had been returned, whose name is Orundellico. (The British call him Jemmy Button, a name that is today seen as demeaning.) He says he has no wish to go back to England, and that evening, they meet his new wife.

The next day, "Every soul on board was heartily sorry to shake hands with him for the last time." Darwin concludes, "I do not now doubt that he will be as happy as, perhaps happier than, if he had never left his own country."

Finally, after more than two years of exploration on South America's Atlantic coast, the *Beagle* passes through the Strait of Magellan and heads for the Pacific. Now young Darwin will have an opportunity to trek in the Andes Mountains and to do some exploring of South America's western coast. (Today these regions are in southern Argentina, Chile, Bolivia, Peru, and Ecuador.)

He is beginning to see a linkage of geography and biology: Could land and sea barriers affect migrations and also life itself? (Darwin keeps track of hummingbird migration patterns in his notes of the *Beagle* voyage.) Might such barriers affect species and how they are formed? Darwin records several species of mice on the eastern side of the Andes Mountains: he finds fewer species on the western side, and they are different from the eastern mice. Fossils he uncovers tell him that different kinds of plants and animals are found at different altitudes.

An illustration of two species of mice from Darwin's Zoology of the Voyage of H.M.S. Beagle

One day, Darwin is napping in the woods in Valdivia, Chile, when the ground begins to move. Later, he writes, "The earth, the very emblem of solidity, has moved beneath our feet like a crust over a fluid." It is a major earthquake, and Darwin is lucky not to have been hurt. He can't confirm it, but he is right about the Earth beneath him; it is crust over a fluid.

The *Beagle* sails north, to the quake's center, which is at Talcahuano, in Chile. Darwin describes what he sees "as if a thousand ships had been wrecked." Darwin is told that the ground opened a foot and then closed back, the sea drained out of Talcahuano Bay, the water turned black, huge whirlpools formed, columns of smoke rose from the sea—and when the water returned, it was in a destructive fury that leveled the inland town of Concepción.

This drawing shows the remains of the cathedral in Concepción after the 1835 earthquake there.

A line of volcanoes stretches for hundreds of miles along South America's Pacific coast; many have erupted in tandem with the earthquake. Darwin now believes the center of the Earth is a rocky furnace and that sometimes hot lava bursts forth from it. "We can scarcely avoid the conclusion, however fearful it may be, that a vast lake of melted matter, of an area nearly doubling in extent that of the Black Sea, is spread out beneath a mere crust of solid land," he writes.

Henslow has sent Darwin the just-published third volume of Lyell's geology series; it arrives by ship. Darwin reads and rereads all three of the books to better understand what he is seeing. He discovers that some coastal land in Chile is now higher than it was before the earthquake. Is this how mountains are formed? Is this what Lyell means when he writes that nature's action, over long periods of time, causes Earth's changes?

The HMS *Beagle* goes on, now to the Galápagos Islands, which straddle the equator some 600 miles (965 kilometers) west of Ecuador. These islands, once a hideout for pirates, are volcanic chimneys. To Darwin, they look like huge iron foundries surrounded by dark waste. He describes the Galápagos as "a little world within itself."

The inhabitants of that little world on the Galápagos include giant tortoises, prickly pear cacti, and three-foot-long (one-meter-long) black iguanas that he says some call "imps of darkness." The iguanas he sees are likely to have yellowish or pinkish chests and gray shoulders. These dark lizards live on rocks of hardened black lava.

Birds that have no fear of humans peck Darwin's fingertips. Darwin has arrived at the right time; a few decades later, the islands will show the impact of human visitors.

Galápagos Islands have similar but not identical environments. Darwin learns that the flora and fauna are not the same on all the islands, and birds and tortoises on one island can differ from those on islands just 20 miles (32 kilometers) away. Species are similar but not exactly the same; and they are different from those on the nearby Ecuadorian mainland.

Most of Darwin's contemporaries, including Lyell, believe that each species of plant and animal is perfectly adapted to its environment. This is part of the accepted belief that every life-form is a unique creation of God made for its time and place on Earth. But why are there subtle differences showing up among species inhabiting neighboring islands? It's baffling. Evolutionary thoughts percolate in Darwin's head, but slowly. His main interest is still geology.

Ashore for five weeks, he collects a variety of birds (actually it is his assistant Syms Covington who does most of the shooting). Darwin dries the birds in the sun, as he learned to do in Edinburgh, then he tosses them in a bag, not thinking to note which came from which island.

An illustration of large ground finches from Darwin's Zoology of the Voyage of H.M.S. Beagle

The Galápagos finches have a variety of beaks, but why? Scholars in England, looking at these specimens, realize that beak size and shape must be related to food resources, which are different on different islands. Later, ornithologist John Gould will be excited by those Galápagos birds, identifying twelve species of finches unknown to Europeans.

Darwin keeps detailed notes. In Great Britain a reading, thinking public is eager to explore, even if only vicariously. Long before he returns to England, Darwin's adventures become well known to a prominent group of naturalists who enthusiastically study the notes and specimens he sends from ports each time the *Beagle*

Drawings from Darwin's Journal of Researches into the Geology and Natural History of the Various Countries Visited by H.M.S. Beagle *show his careful study of finch heads and beaks.*

docks. Those British scholars, among the best in the world, expand on his work and delve further into the specimens he has found.

Author Alan Moorehead describes Darwin near the end of the voyage: "He had grown shabbier. One by one the elegant waistcoats and fine white shirts . . . had been mended, patched and finally discarded. He was now rigged out more as a sailor."

His cabin, which he shares with two others, has become a laboratory, crammed with insects, bird skins, dried snakes, and other specimens, along with his microscope and dissecting instruments. He has had five years to turn himself into a working scientist. He will spend the rest of his life making sense of what he has learned. ■

Darwin's Big Idea

As Darwin now conceived it, natural selection operated on living beings as if it were a statistical necessity, a law of nature stripped of any divine influences, invincible, predominant, and fierce, relentlessly honing animals, plants, and humans in the struggle for existence.

—Janet Browne

Evolution by natural selection is the process which accounts for the history of living nature, including human nature. It is arguably the most important idea in the history of the natural and the human sciences.

—Robert M. Young

Charles Darwin, photographed in 1869 by Julia Margaret Cameron

The physical vigor that Darwin displayed during the *Beagle* voyage fades during the years after he returns, as he struggles with ill health. He will never travel again.

For the rest of his life, in his home office and in his garden and greenhouse, he works hard, studying barnacles, pigeons, beetles, birds, and orchids. A studious researcher, he will write a 684-page monograph on barnacles and more on other forms of life.

Now that he's back in England, his family connections and his sojourn as a student at Cambridge give him access to Britain's scientific elite. Richard Owen, Britain's authority on dinosaurs, will study the mammal fossils he has brought home; museum curator George Waterhouse will look at his insects and at his bones from living mammal species. And ornithologist John Gould will begin to make sense of Darwin's bird specimens.

The ornithologist John Gould

It is Gould who realizes that each bird species in Darwin's Galápagos collection has come from a different island. Darwin will remember that the vice governor of the islands told him that the tortoises are different on different islands as well. He will obsess about that and write his thoughts in notebooks. If each life-form is a perfect creation, then why are they not all the same?

For three years after his return, he works relentlessly: classifying specimens, writing of his adventures, and trying to understand what it is that he has uncovered. During that time, he marries his cousin Emma Wedgwood, and they move into a house in London. There he takes his notes and his expanded view of the world and attempts to put them in order.

In his personal notebooks he tries to make sense of what Gould and Owen have seen in his specimens, and what his own observations tell him. He writes a book that he hopes will put him into the ranks of popular explorers, using his hero Alexander von Humboldt as a role model. In 1839, when *The Voyage of the* Beagle is published, it turns, like Humboldt's book, into a best-selling true adventure story, inspiring a generation of armchair and actual adventurers. The second revised edition of the book, published in 1845, becomes a world classic.

By 1842, he and Emma are living in a big comfortable house in the village of Downe, less than 20 miles (32 kilometers) south of London. Ten Darwin children will slide down the house's banisters and play hopscotch on its grounds. Darwin describes the house to his sister in a letter: "The charm of the place to me is that almost every field is intersected . . . by one or more foot-paths—I never saw so many walks in any other country."

Meanwhile, the transmutation (or evolution) problem that eluded his grandfather continues to obsess him. He is critical of his grandfather's work, which he says is too

Darwin's house in the village of Downe

speculative. Charles is determined to prove his own ideas with specifics. But this evolutionary thought emerges slowly; he understands the social, political, and religious implications of a theory that makes *nature* life's creator, an idea that is sure to meet resistance from many clergymen and others in a religious society whose monarch is the head of the national church.

The "species problem" is also obsessing both those who explain nature's changes as divine interventions and those who search for answers through the scientific method of experimentation, which includes controlled research and proof. Neither group can explain life's diversity. Again, if species are perfectly adapted to their environments (as most people believe), why is there more than one kind of snake, or butterfly, or orchid, or finch?

Some say that while each form of plant and animal was created separately, over the long expanse of Earth's history, a limited amount of variety has evolved, creating sibling species, like different varieties of finches. Those who hold this conviction see no connection between different life-forms. That means no connection between fish and reptiles, and certainly no connection between apes and humans.

But there are still baffling questions to be answered. All vertebrates—rats and humans, for example—have similar body layouts, with heart and lungs and veins. Doesn't that suggest kinship? If so, how has it happened?

It is clear to Darwin that species are related to one another, but how? Darwin is familiar with animal and plant breeders who select favorable traits when they appear naturally, breed for them, and often come up with new and desirable variations. This has been done with roses, dogs, and horses. That controlled breeding process is known as "artificial selection." Could nature be doing the same thing on its own in a process of natural selection?

Darwin reads everything pertinent he can find. Most thinkers of his time have rejected Erasmus's transmutation thesis. That includes the well-known polymath William Whewell (pronounced HYOO-ul), a Cambridge professor who is president of the Geological Society. Whewell has coined the word *scientist* to describe those who

A portrait of William Whewell

have previously been known as natural philosophers. In 1837, Whewell writes, "Species have a real existence in nature, and a transmutation from one to another does not exist." Which means, according to this expert: there is no evolution.

In a notebook meant only for himself, Darwin challenges the great Whewell when he writes, "Each species changes."

When he reads Thomas Malthus's *Essay on the Principle of Population*, Darwin is astonished. Malthus, another well-known Cambridge man, has found that the natural tendency of populations of most living things is to increase geometrically. A geometric (also called exponential) progression is 1, 2, 4, 8, 16, 32, 64, etc., with each number *double* that of the number before. That means a population of two rabbits, for instance, can grow to thousands of rabbits within a few generations. Darwin is not a great mathematician, but the math of doubling makes sense to him. And its implication—when you think of the growth of species—is awesome. He realizes that most human populations, expanding exponentially, will double every twenty-five years. That means the descendants of a single pair of any species—left unchecked—could soon cover the world.

But that doesn't happen. Why not? That question stays in his mind. Darwin is now making notes in his notebook about "my theory."

Three species of jackrabbits, from a 1907 book on evolution in animals

Slowly, slowly, his theory comes into focus. It begins with the understanding that children are not exact copies, or clones, of their parents. That idea will be called "descent with modification." It is just an acknowledgment that change happens naturally. Each generation is unique. Which means modifications are a regular part of the life process. Some changes are of no consequence, some are major, some are harmful, and a few are terrific. Darwin doesn't know what creates change. He just knows change happens.

And he knows that those modifications may be inherited. While change seems random, changes that work well are likely to get passed on to future generations. Some individuals and some species make it, and some don't. Those that are best adapted are most likely to survive and have more offspring. Those that are poorly adapted don't. All this takes vast time, but thanks to the geologists of the day, Darwin can now think in terms of an ancient Earth.

Over thousands of generations, small adaptations, one after another, become significant. They can lead to new species. So change happens, and change may be random, but selection is not: it is a response to the demands of the world. The term Darwin uses for this idea is "natural selection" (meaning nature does the selecting), and it is now also known as "Darwinian evolution."

Then, Darwin writes, the "whole fabric totters & falls." The whole fabric he is talking about is the theology that is the backbone of British society. "But Man—wonderful Man is an exception," he writes in his private notebook. He can't, however, sustain that thought. A few lines later he writes, "He is no exception." The implication of that thought is that people are part of the animal kingdom and not that special.

The skulls of four different primates: a human, a chimpanzee, an orangutan, and a macaque

Meanwhile, he reads *Vestiges of the Natural History of Creation*, a book that is getting a lot of attention because it focuses on the "development hypothesis," the idea that one species may transmute (or change) into another. Anonymously written by Robert Chambers, a book publisher, *Vestiges* goes through several printings and is very controversial, even among scientists, many of whom criticize its lack of rigor. But it is an international best-seller and is even read by Queen Victoria.

Vestiges doesn't offer a solid explanation for transmutation, and Darwin has mixed feelings about the book because of some of its errors, but he will come to believe that it creates an audience for a more detailed and insightful work on the subject.

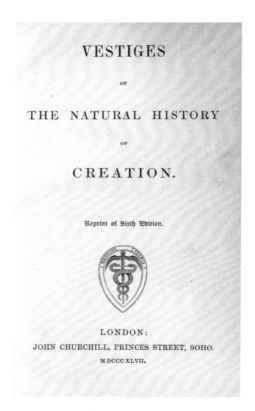

A biology bestseller of its day

The book's author, Robert Chambers, circa 1864

Darwin is working on such a book, but he isn't ready to publish. He believes he doesn't have enough documentation for his ideas; he knows evolution is a divisive subject, and he hasn't quite nailed down the process by which it happens. He also worries about upsetting his devout wife. She believes, as he once did, that every creature is an independent and perfect creation. Darwin is now doing a back-and-forth dance in his mind trying to reconcile conflicting ideas.

The Malay Archipelago is the huge group of islands between mainland Southeast Asia and Australia. It includes Indonesia, the Philippines, and Singapore.

Meanwhile, someone who has read Humboldt, Lyell, Malthus, *Vestiges*, and *The Voyage of the* Beagle, who has gone exploring in South America and in the Malay Archipelago, has come up with an explanation of how evolution works. He has an article ready to be published. But first this man, Alfred Russel Wallace (1823–1913), sends his explanation to Darwin, whom he greatly admires. ■

The Other Guy

09

In science the credit goes to the man who convinces the world, not to the man to whom the idea first occurs.

—Francis Darwin

Mr. Darwin has given to the world a new science, and his name should, in my opinion, stand above that of every philosopher of ancient or modern times. The force of admiration can no further go!!!

—Alfred Russel Wallace

British naturalist Alfred Russel Wallace, circa 1895

We know who Mr. Darwin is, but who is Mr. Wallace?

He has sent his own evolutionary ideas in an 1858 letter to Darwin from Ternate, a cone-shaped island that is the world's largest producer of cloves. Ternate and its neighbors have long been known in Europe as the Spice Islands and today are part of Indonesia.

Wallace could have sent his letter, with thoughts on life and its process of change, to a learned society to publish, but he chose, perhaps naively, to send the paper to a man he admires: Charles Darwin. He asks Darwin to share it with Britain's leading geologist, Charles Lyell, whom Darwin knows well.

Wallace is fourteen years younger than Darwin. He was raised in a middle-class home, where, every evening, his father read aloud to his nine children. The family struggled financially, but Wallace says, "Through reading clubs or lending libraries we usually had some of the best books of travel or biography in the house."

At fourteen, he leaves school because he needs to earn a living. In the years that follow, he supports himself as a surveyor (taught by an older brother) and a teacher of drawing, mapmaking, and surveying at the Collegiate School in Leicester. In that town's fine library, Wallace meets a young entomologist, Henry Walter Bates. They share a fascination for nature, and they both love collecting bugs, butterflies, and interesting plants. Bates, who has some expertise in the field, gives Wallace tips on how to become a professional collector. Wallace soon has a collecting bottle, pins, a beetle box, and a manual on British bugs.

Cloves are flower buds that are often used as a spice and as a flavoring in some toothpastes; they have antibacterial properties and can also decrease inflammation for people who have maladies like arthritis.

Clove blossoms and dried buds

These two young men, both serious readers, also spend a lot of time talking about books. Like Darwin, they read Humboldt, Lyell, Malthus, and *Vestiges of the Natural History of Creation*, the controversial book that has everyone arguing about the evolution idea. Both also read and admire Darwin's *The Voyage of the* Beagle.

When they are apart, Wallace and Bates send letters to each other. "I begin to feel rather dissatisfied with a mere local collection," Wallace writes. "I should like to take some one [plant or animal] family to study thoroughly, principally with a view to the theory of the origin of species." It's twelve years before Darwin will write a book with that very title.

Wallace is taking *Vestiges* seriously and wants to see if he can prove some of its ideas, especially those on trans- mutation. In 1845, in a letter to Bates, he says:

English entomologist Henry Walter Bates

> I have a rather more favourable opinion of the 'Vestiges' than you appear to have. I do not consider it a hasty gener- alization, but rather as an ingenious hypothesis strongly supported by some striking facts and analogies, but which remains to be proven by more facts and the additional light which more research may throw upon the problem. It furnishes a subject for every student of nature to attend to.

Some of Bates's field journals

Wallace now has a goal: to prove the "ingenious hypothesis," by which he means the evolutionary concept articulated in the *Vestiges* and by Lamarck and Erasmus Darwin. To do that, he needs to gather data, and he wants to collect it in South America.

The two young naturalists go to the British Museum and ask for advice on how to pay for a trip to South America. They are told that any animals, birds, and insects they collect will find eager buyers and that should cover their expenses. When, in April of 1848, an agent agrees to handle sales for them, they sail for Brazil.

Bates and Wallace begin their South American sojourn at Pará, a part of modern-day Brazil close to the mouth of the Amazon, then they head in different directions into the rain forest. Each will explore, pack up specimens, and send them home.

A cock of the rock

Spotting a gorgeous bird on a stony outcrop, Wallace describes it as "shining out like a mass of brilliant flame." The scarlet bird (scientifically *Rupicola rupicola*) is now known as "cock of the rock." Wallace sends two dozen of those gorgeous red birds home to England. Darwin, who had no need to make money, usually collected one example of a species. Wallace, thinking of sales, collects many.

In 1852, preparing to come home, Wallace fills six big crates with specimens. He also packs a live menagerie of five monkeys, two macaws, and more than twenty other birds, along with his journals, notes, and drawings. All are loaded on a small ship, the *Helen*. After three weeks at sea, the *Helen* catches fire and sinks. Wallace and the crew escape in an open lifeboat. Marooned in the mid-ocean Sargasso Sea, they are picked up by a rescue ship, which itself almost sinks. After four years in the Amazon, Wallace comes home with only a few notebooks to document his adventure; he says he will never travel again.

Wallace soon changes his mind, however. He is thirty-one upon his return, an experienced naturalist, and despite his earlier travails, he is once again itching to do more exploring. His wise agent insured the lost cargo, so Wallace has the means to live in

London. He writes papers on biology. Those papers, and some specimens he sent to London on other ships, give him stature in the collecting world. He briefly meets the now well-known Charles Darwin. In 1854, Wallace's connections get him free passage on a steamship heading for Singapore. From there he travels to Sarawak, on the northwestern coast of the island of Borneo.

Later, Wallace writes, "I was to begin the eight years of wandering throughout the Malay Archipelago, which constituted the central and controlling incident of my life." He sends a groundbreaking paper from Sarawak to *The Annals and Magazine of Natural History* that is published in 1855. In that paper he says, "Every species has come into existence coincident . . . with a pre-existing closely-allied species." Today that principle is known as the Sarawak Law. It says that life-forms don't just appear; they aren't random. They are connected to other forms of life.

Charles Lyell is influenced by Wallace's paper. He has been an opponent of previous concepts of transmutation and evolution, but Wallace's paper seems to have him reconsidering. He starts keeping his own notebooks on species changes.

It takes years for Darwin to accept the idea that change (or evolution) is part of the life process; Wallace begins with that idea. He calls it the "progressive development of plants and

Species and Specimens

When Henry Bates arrives home in 1859 after more than a decade on the Amazon, he brings specimens of more than fourteen thousand species, mostly insects, eight thousand of them new to science. And in 1862, when Wallace comes home from Malaysia, he brings two live birds-of-paradise with him. On the voyage home, he stops in Malta, where he collects cockroaches for the birds to eat.

According to Michael Shermer's *In Darwin's Shadow*, Wallace also brings an "almost unimaginable 125,660 specimens, including 310 mammals, 100 reptiles, 8,050 birds, 7,500 shells, 13,100 butterflies, 83,200 beetles, and 13,400 other insects, over a thousand of which were new species." Bates and Wallace will each write a popular book about their adventures.

animals," but he doesn't know how that development happens. Is it just chance, or is there more to nature's changes?

In Malaysia, Wallace studies a gorgeous butterfly, then he finds that on neighboring islands, the same type of butterfly has slightly different characteristics. The islands have similar environments. If all life-forms are perfectly designed for their environment, why aren't the butterflies all the same? It is the same question Darwin asked about finches and iguanas in the Galápagos Islands. Why aren't they all the same from island to island?

Malaysian butterflies from a book by Alfred Russel Wallace

Wallace believes the butterflies are all descendants of a common ancestor. What has caused their differences? If there is a process of change embedded in nature, how does it work? Wallace is trying to figure that out.

Charles Lyell realizes that Wallace is getting close to unraveling the puzzle of the origin of species. Lyell knows that Darwin is working on that same puzzle and writes to him, "I wish you would publish some small fragment of your data, pigeons if you please, and so out with the theory and let it take date and be cited and understood." He wants Darwin to establish his priority in what may become a race to see who will be first to solve the species problem.

But Darwin is an obsessive researcher, and he says he isn't ready. He is very aware of the criticisms of *Vestiges* and of his grandfather. Neither of those thinkers had solid facts to support his ideas. He replies to Lyell, "With respect to your suggestion of a sketch of my view, I hardly know what to think, but will reflect on it; but it goes against my prejudices. To give a fair sketch would be impossible, for every proposition requires such an array of facts."

Darwin wants to get things right and document his theory with specifics. He spends years studying barnacles—not just living barnacles but fossilized ones too. He wants to master the biological history of a single group of interrelated species so he can understand how they have changed over time. He doesn't want any doubts before he publishes a theory. He tells Lyell that the big book he's working on will take longer to finish than he anticipated.

Darwin hesitates; he says he needs more time. By 1856, it is almost twenty years since his return home on the *Beagle*. Does he have a theory explaining how new species evolve or has he hit a dead end? There is controversy about that. Recent research into postal records shows that a letter addressed to Darwin from Wallace in the Malay Archipelago arrived on January 12, 1857. Four months later, on May 1, Darwin answers that letter, saying he received it "a few days ago." Was that just carelessness or was Darwin trying to conceal the impact of Wallace's thoughts? Was he stalling for time? Or are the postal dates wrong?

An illustration from Darwin's book on barnacles

Still, Darwin's notes indicate that his theorizing about evolution started as early as 1838. While he has been going slowly, amassing evidence and writing in detail, Wallace is doing fieldwork and delving into biogeography. Here is how Wallace will later describe his research:

> The problem then was, not only how and why do species change, but how and why do they change into new and well-defined species . . . why and how do they become so exactly adapted to distinct modes of life; and why do all the intermediate grades die out (as geology shows they have died out). . . . It then occurred to me that . . . the destruction every year . . . must be enormous in order to keep down the numbers of each species, since evidently they do not increase regularly from year to year, as otherwise the world would long ago have been crowded with those that breed most quickly. Vaguely thinking over the enormous and constant destruction . . . it occurred to me to ask the question, Why do some die and some live? And the answer was clearly, that on the whole the best fitted live. . . . [T]hus the definite characters and the clear isolation of each new species would be explained.

In February 1858, Wallace, who has continued his correspondence with Darwin, puts many of his ideas into the paper he sends to Darwin in a letter from Ternate. In it, he describes what will become known as "natural selection," a term Darwin first used in 1844 in an unpublished essay in which he says that nature has a selection process.

Darwin realizes that he is no longer alone in his thinking. "Even his terms stand as heads of my chapters," he writes after receiving the letter from Wallace.

Did two great minds come to similar conclusions at about the same time? Or should one of them get more credit than the other?

That debate continues today. In a 2008 book, Roy Davies will accuse Darwin of committing "one of the greatest thefts of intellectual property in the history of science." In other words, he thinks Darwin stole the natural selection idea from Wallace. But that is not the prevailing view among scholars; a 2011 study published in the *Biological Journal of the Linnean Society* examined the timing of letters between Wallace and Darwin and found that Darwin was "vindicated from accusations of deceit."

There is also a difference between the ideas of these two scientific giants. For Darwin, natural selection is random and chancy, but for Wallace, evolution has purpose and design. Those two different worldviews continue to exist today.

When Darwin reads Wallace's paper, he is dismayed. Wallace has come up with an explanation for species change much like the one he himself has been working on for many years. Wallace has asked Darwin to show his paper to Charles Lyell. What shall he do?

Darwin doesn't want to be unfair or ungentlemanly. But he wants credit for discovering natural selection. He turns to Lyell for advice. They both know that if Wallace's paper is published first, Wallace will become known as the one who has solved the species problem.

In answering Wallace, Darwin says, "I can plainly see that we have thought much alike and to a certain extent have come to similar conclusions."

Lyell concocts a plan. He thinks he can help Darwin and also do right by Wallace. ∎

Three Papers and an Entangled Bank

10

Truth is born into this world only with pangs and tribulations, and every fresh truth is received unwillingly. To expect the world to receive a new truth, or even an old truth, without challenging it, is to look for one of those miracles which do not occur.

—Alfred Russel Wallace

The publication of the Darwin and Wallace papers in 1858, and still more that of the "Origin" in 1859, had the effect . . . of the flash of light, which to a man who has lost himself in a dark night, suddenly reveals a road which, whether it takes him straight home or not, certainly goes his way. . . .

My reflection, when I first made myself master of the central idea of the "Origin," was, "How extremely stupid not to have thought of that!"

—Thomas Henry Huxley

A 1786 painting of an English riverbank by Joseph Wright

When the great Swedish taxonomist Linnaeus dies, his papers need to go somewhere. So the Linnean Society is created in London to house them. (Today the society can be found on Piccadilly Street, at comfortable Burlington House, next to the Geological Society, where it quietly thrives.) Seventy years later, in May 1859, the organization is old and prestigious when its president, Thomas Bell, gives the customary annual overview of the year's scientific events. In that speech, Bell says, "The year which has passed has not, indeed, been marked by any of those striking discoveries which at once revolutionize . . . brilliant innovation."

The Linnean Society's coat of arms

Hindsight, of course, provides the perfect vantage point from which to see how very wrong he was. We now know that three papers read aloud at the Linnean Society on July 1, 1858, to "thirty-odd nonplussed fellows" are as brilliantly innovative as science gets. They are the first public statement of what comes to be known as the theory of evolution, or, often, Darwinian evolution. That 1858 reading is *the* most revolutionary and brilliant moment in the Linnean Society's history. Nothing before or since has come close to matching it.

Written by Alfred Russel Wallace and Charles Darwin, the papers address the species problem, or how new species originate—and come up with the same answer. Wallace's paper is titled "On the Tendency of Varieties to Depart Indefinitely from the Original Type." Darwin's ideas are presented in two papers, one an extract from an unpublished essay written in 1844, the other an abstract of an 1857 letter to Harvard professor Asa Gray. Presenting these papers is seen by Lyell as a way to help his friend Darwin. Wallace is thrilled when he learns of the pairing.

The papers are statements of the same basic idea: that all life on Earth has evolved over a long period of time from an ancestral pool that produced, and continues to produce, variations; it is the fittest of those variations that survive and reproduce. Behind that simple concept is this fundamental one: all life on Earth is related and subject to the same processes.

But when the papers are read—and this idea explained in the words of both authors—the Linnean Society members don't seem to get it. They don't disagree; like President Bell, they seem to have missed the point. And neither Darwin nor Wallace is there for the reading.

The Nature of Natural Selection

"Natural selection as proposed by Darwin and Wallace was a most novel and daring theory," biologist Ernst Mayr will write in 2001, adding that in his view it was "based on five observations (facts) and three inferences." (An inference is a conclusion that can be reached after research and observation.) Mayr's summary of the facts and inferences are listed below, with some editing:

Fact 1: Left alone, populations of plants and animals will increase exponentially.

Fact 2: In the real world, population size tends to remain relatively stable over time.

Fact 3: Resources available to all species are limited.

Inference 1: There is intense competition and a struggle for existence among the members of a species.

Fact 4: No two individuals in a population are exactly the same.

Inference 2: The likelihood of survival differs among individuals.

Fact 5: Many of those differences among individuals are at least partly based on inherited traits.

Inference 3: Natural selection, over many generations, results in evolution.

In an article written later, Alfred Newton, a Cambridge professor of anatomy, claims that he understood the impact at the time:

> *Not many days after my return home there reached me the part of the Journal of the Linnean Society which bears on its cover the date 20th August 1858, and contains the papers by Mr Darwin and Mr Wallace. . . . I sat up late that night to read it; and never shall I forget the impression it made upon me.*

He wrote that the papers "contained a perfectly simple solution of all the difficulties which had been troubling me for months past," adding, "I never doubted for one moment, then nor since, that we had one of the grandest discoveries of the age—a discovery all the more grand because it was so simple."

But the papers Darwin and Wallace produce are not widely available. Outside of a small section of the scientific elite, no one has yet heard of their evolutionary idea. If this idea is to find its footing, it needs a detailed and understandable explanation—and it doesn't get that at the Linnean Society. Charles Darwin will provide that understanding in a popular book to come.

Darwin has not been in a hurry to tell the world about the ideas that have been filling his head for the twenty years since his *Beagle* voyage. Mostly he has been immersed in scholarly research. But the realization that other naturalists—namely Wallace—are coming to the same conclusions helps spur him on. He moves to publish his book laying out his idea of natural selection in 1859. He intends to explain his evolutionary thesis to a broad audience—and to back up his argument with proof.

That book, titled *On the Origin of Species by Means of Natural Selection, or the Preservation of Favoured Races in the Struggle for Life* (usually shortened to *On the Origin of Species*), challenges the way most people think of life. The basic idea of Darwin's book, like many great ideas, is simple: life-forms change over time and can't all survive; those that are best adapted to their surroundings are most likely to live longer and reproduce. Stated another way: as long as there is variation in life-forms, those with the most advantageous variations will be most likely to propagate.

ON

THE ORIGIN OF SPECIES

BY MEANS OF NATURAL SELECTION,

OR THE

PRESERVATION OF FAVOURED RACES IN THE STRUGGLE
FOR LIFE.

By CHARLES DARWIN, M.A.,

FELLOW OF THE ROYAL, GEOLOGICAL, LINNÆAN, ETC., SOCIETIES;
AUTHOR OF 'JOURNAL OF RESEARCHES DURING H. M. S. BEAGLE'S VOYAGE
ROUND THE WORLD.'

LONDON:
JOHN MURRAY, ALBEMARLE STREET.
1859.

The right of Translation is reserved.

The title page of Darwin's most famous work

That idea, now known as Darwinism or natural selection, explains what had been unexplainable: how life evolves over time. What Darwin can't explain is how those changes happen.

The poet Alfred, Lord Tennyson, a peer of Darwin's, describes nature as "red in tooth and claw." Darwin buys that concept of nature as a battlefield, but he finds much more than violence there. He ends *Origin of Species* with a famous passage that attempts to portray the interwoven complexity of many natural environments:

> *Who trusted God was love indeed*
> *And love Creation's final law—*
> *Tho' Nature, red in tooth and claw*
> *With ravine, shriek'd against his creed.*
>
> *—Alfred, Lord Tennyson*

Did Darwin have a real entangled bank in mind when he wrote the ending to *On the Origin of Species*? His great-great-grandson Randal Keynes believes he did. Family documents, studied by Keynes, cite a hillock called Orchis Bank, in Kent, near Darwin's home.

> *It is interesting to contemplate an entangled bank, clothed with many plants of many kinds, with birds singing on the bushes, with various insects flitting about, and with worms crawling through the damp earth, and to reflect that these elaborately constructed forms, so different from each other, and dependent upon each other in so complex a manner, have all been produced by laws acting around us.*

When Darwin writes "by laws acting around us," he is saying that nature has its own rules (or laws) that create change, and we humans should try to understand them. Isaac Newton, with his law of gravity, has made the idea of natural laws acceptable. For Darwin, natural selection is nature's key law, and it will provide a foundation for the expanded biological sciences to come. Some of Darwin's specifics won't hold up—just as Newton's law of gravity will be nudged by Albert Einstein's theory of general relativity. But Darwin's big thought, that nature follows rules—the same idea that guided Isaac Newton and Albert Einstein—will prevail. And if life, as Darwin says, is directed by actual laws, those laws and processes need to be discovered and studied if we are to understand it.

Published in 1859, a year after Darwin's and Wallace's papers were read at the Linnean Society, *On the Origin of Species* lands like an explosive in the sedate and walled British intellectual world. The book seems scandalous to most British citizens and others who have accepted a world of nature with God as the active decision maker and humans as God's unique creation.

Some others are eager to pick a fight with England's established church and its hold on the great universities. Brilliant, self-educated Thomas Huxley, who calls himself "Darwin's bulldog," coins the word *agnostic*, which refers to someone who is undecided about the existence of God. A member of the London School Board, Huxley helps change curricula by adding more science.

Is Darwin fair to Wallace? That question is the subject of continued debate. In the first edition of his book, Darwin writes of "my theory" dozens of times (in later editions that phrase appears less frequently). Although he does cite Wallace and his work in the first edition, he ignores the contributions of his grandfather Erasmus and of Lamarck, though he will later mention them in a preface.

Publicly, Darwin shares credit for the idea of natural selection with Wallace, but *On the Origin of Species* is Darwin's work, and it is this book that is widely discussed and ultimately game changing.

An 1899 illustration entitled The Last Stand—Science versus Superstition

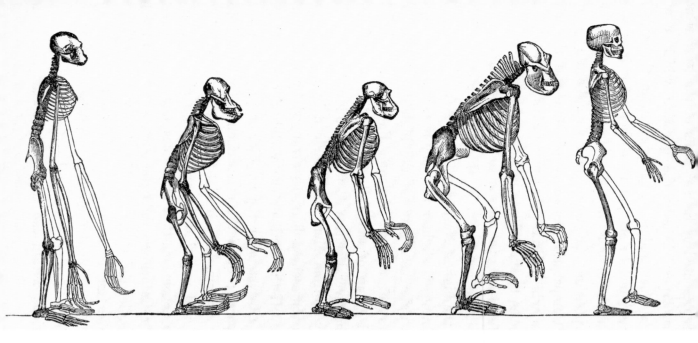

This drawing from an 1879 book on evolution shows the skeletons of a gibbon, orangutan, chimpanzee, gorilla, and human.

When Darwin's polymath friend Herbert Spencer reads *On the Origin of Species*, he comes up with the phrase "survival of the fittest" to describe its theme, referring to plants and animals best adapted to live in their surroundings. In the fifth edition of his book, Darwin will adopt "survival of the fittest" as a synonym for natural selection. Wallace actually prefers it to "natural selection," a term that has long been used by breeders of animals. But they are both clear that it is the fittest who are able to reproduce through a selection process that is often cruel and competitive.

Herbert Spencer envisions the idea of survival of the fittest being applied far beyond biology. While Darwin focuses on how species adapt to specific environments over time, Spencer deploys Darwin's ideas to the competition within human society, both among individuals and races. Called "social Darwinism," the grim idea purports that certain superior people and societies are destined to rule over, and even exploit, others.

In years to come, social Darwinism will take Darwin's ideas and use them to justify deadly prejudices. For example, a practice known as eugenics is aimed at reshaping human populations by controlling who gets to have children. (The word *eugenics* is coined by Francis Galton, a cousin of Darwin.) It is an attempt to improve the genetic stock of humanity, in the way farmers breed cattle and other animals. Humans, of course, are not livestock, and these ideas lead to the mass murder of entire groups of people whom people in power want to exploit or scapegoat.

What does Darwin himself make of these ideas? That is a controversial topic. While Darwin abhors slavery, in his book *The Descent of Man, and Selection in Relation to Sex*, published a dozen years after *Origin of Species*, he takes a hierarchical view of human societies. Europeans, he writes, "stand at the summit of civilisation." He even claims, with specious evidence, that Europeans have the largest brains.

Where all this will lead is not clear at the time, but the perversion of evolutionary theories into racial and ethnic pronouncements takes root. Eugenics becomes popular in Europe and America in the early twentieth century, leading to the murderous and racist ideology of the Nazi Party in Germany in the 1930s and 1940s. After World War II, it will be discredited and found to be based on racism, not science. But the pernicious ideas associated with eugenics will not disappear entirely.

Darwin's discoveries about biology and evolution are as profound as those of Galileo when he announced that the sun, the Earth, and the whole universe respond to laws of mathematics and was put on trial by the Catholic Church. Part of the reason for the Church's disapproval: Galileo wrote with clarity, making sure that ordinary people could read and understand what he had to say.

Like Galileo, Darwin writes clearly. *On the Origin of Species* turns out to be a literary masterpiece and a best-seller. Written for non-specialists, it will persuade generations of readers. And provoke many too—even many who never read it.

Darwin isn't surprised. In the 1859 edition of *Origin*, he writes:

When the views entertained in this volume on the origin of species, or when analogous views are generally admitted, we can dimly foresee that there will be a considerable revolution in natural history.

"Considerable revolution"? This book will transform how we understand the natural world and ourselves. ■

Mendel Minding Peas

11

A still life of peas and plums by Polish painter Mateusz Tokarski

Why, given the same parents, might one child have blue eyes and her brother brown? Why does a large-boned foal appear in a breed of small horses? Darwin doesn't know. No one does.

Most people in the nineteenth century think that offspring inherit an average of their parents' characteristics. It is called "blending theory." But if that were true, unusual characteristics would gradually disappear—no one would be very tall or very short. Everyone would be in a blended middle. That isn't what happens. Why?

This isn't just a question for the curious. For people who raise animals or grow fruit trees, understanding and then controlling inheritance offers tantalizing possibilities. Imagine being able to breed sheep that produce extra-thick coats of wool. Or trees that are extra heavy with juicy fruit. Farmers and animal breeders have been doing experimental mating through much of agricultural history; by the middle of the nineteenth century, questions of breeding and inheritance are being seriously considered in the university world as well as by those who tend gardens or raise chickens or hogs.

In the Austrian village of Brünn (today known as Brno, in what is now the Czech Republic), a Catholic friar who is immersed in agriculture asks himself questions about inheritance. Is there a pattern to inheritance? Can it be tracked from one generation to another?

The friar asking these questions is Gregor Mendel (1822–1884). A quiet fellow, he will manage to study with some of the great minds in the German-speaking scientific community of his time. And he will begin to unravel the secrets of inheritance.

In Brünn, two rivers come together, and a castle and a great cathedral dominate the

You can call animal herders and farmers the first geneticists and not be wrong. They learned to control animal and plant breeding in order to produce traits that seemed desirable (such as speed, or strength). Ancient farmers learned to be selective when they planted seeds. Farmers in Mexico and other parts of the Americas spent thousands of years developing corn from a wild grass. Chinese farmers began cultivating rice ten thousand years ago, gradually breeding preferred traits to make it the robust crop it is today.

skyline. It's a town with a tradition of scholarship and good schools, but most of those who live there and below the hills, in the neighboring flatland, are concerned with agriculture: growing crops, tending fruit trees, or raising animals.

As for our friar, born Johann Mendel in 1822 (which makes him thirteen years younger than Darwin), he is the son of Anton and Rosine Mendel, hardworking peasant farmers who grow fruit trees. Anton Mendel works with a local priest who is an expert gardener to improve the yields and hardiness of the trees he grows. He is able to use grafts from the orchards of a nearby manor. Johann, a thoughtful lad, loves working with his father and becomes fascinated with studying the natural world.

Gregor Mendel, friar and scientist

For most peasant children, school lasts only a few years. But it is clear to everyone that Johann has an unusual mind. He studies at a school in a neighboring town, but his parents' money is spread thin. If he is to eat, he must tutor other students; shy Johann sometimes goes hungry. Still, he is determined to get an education. He has big ideas, which he explains in a poem he writes in his native German:

> *May the might of destiny grant me*
> *The supreme ecstasy of earthly joy,*
> *The highest goal of earthly ecstasy,*
> *That of seeing, when I arise from the tomb,*
> *My art thriving peacefully,*
> *Among those who come after me.*

Grafting is a way to produce plants from pieces of existing plants instead of from seeds. This technique can speed up the growing process and allows farmers to mix the root systems of hardy plants with the high-quality branches of another, similar plant. This is most typically done with plants of the same species, though it can sometimes work if they are from different species. Branches or buds are cut, for example, from one tomato plant that produces particularly juicy tomatoes and are placed on another tomato plant, where they fuse together.

This 1855 painting by French artist Jean-François Millet depicts a farmer inserting a graft onto a tree.

Johann does well in school and earns money by tutoring. But after his father has an accident and can no longer work, his parents are unable to give him any financial help at all. He goes to study at the Philosophical Institute at Olmütz; he is helped by one of his sisters.

The primary language at the school in Olmütz is Czech. Mendel can speak Czech but not well enough to tutor in it. He heads home, where there is food to eat, but he struggles with depression. He takes to his bed and stays there for most of a year.

A teacher suggests he enter the Abbey of Saint Thomas in nearby Brünn and become a friar. When he does, in 1843, he is expected to take a new name, and he becomes Gregor.

He has chosen his path well. The abbey, a brick building originally built to house nuns, sits among rolling hills speckled with fruit trees. Walls that once separated nuns' cells have been torn down, creating rooms for the priests. The abbey is known for training cooks; skinny Mendel finally has enough

The Abbey of Saint Thomas in Brünn

to eat. A fine library near the bedrooms provides intellectual food. Mendel has found a home where he can devote himself to his two passions: gardening and scholarship.

The friars follow the Latin credo of Saint Augustine: *Per scientiam ad sapientiam*, "From knowledge to wisdom." In contrast to some orders, where monks cloister themselves in monasteries of focused devotion, the friars at Saint Thomas's work in service to the lay community.

What will Mendel contribute to the community? The scholarly abbot, Cyril Napp, suggests that he become a schoolteacher and sends him to study for a degree at the University of Vienna. Mendel is lucky. German universities are leading much of the world, especially in science. Christian Doppler, who will become known for his identification of a sound wave phenomenon to be called the Doppler effect, is among his professors. Other teachers have renown in biology and physics. Mendel studies and is fascinated by a new branch of mathematics that we now call statistics. Probability and statistics will be critical components of the work he is going to do.

Probability deals with how likely an event is to occur—usually measured by the ratio of actual cases to the number of possible cases. For example, the probability that you will roll the number three on a six-sided die is 1 in 6. As for statistics, it is a type of mathematics that involves the collection, organization, and analysis of data.

Now, with the church paying his bills, Mendel has what he needs to be comfortable. But as a student, he has new problems. It may be a fear of tests. He keeps failing the exams he needs to pass to get a degree. He will eventually manage to teach in a high school, but without some of the credentials that he is expected to have.

Back at the abbey, he builds beehives in order to study bees (and enjoy their honey); he will also delve into astronomy and meteorology. But Mendel knows what he really wants to do, which is to follow his father in trying to make plants more productive. Mendel hopes to study inheritance in nature so he can understand how traits are passed from parent to child or from tree to seedling.

Abbott Napp, who seems to appreciate the promise of his shy friar, encourages Mendel to pursue his interest in science. At first Mendel tries breeding mice in cages in his room, but that upsets a bishop who comes for a visit, because the mice smell. Abbott Napp adds a long glass-roofed greenhouse to the monastery, where Mendel can grow plants and learn from them. Mendel knows that in the seventeenth century, Isaac Newton and Gottfried Leibniz realized that mathematical rules and ratios govern the physical world. Mendel intends to see if math and ratios might govern heredity in the plant world.

He searches for a plant that can be easily bred and documented, and finds that the ordinary garden pea (*Pisum sativum*) is just right. This is not a random choice. Some German scientists have done work with peas; they have proved to be an ideal plant for experimentation. The blossom of *Pisum sativum* is structured in a way that keeps out wind-blown pollen and bees, which might randomly pollinate plants, and these peas can self-fertilize, which means they have both male and female parts and don't need another plant to reproduce. Without interference from outside factors, the garden pea breeds true, which means that breeding them is likely to give simple, straightforward results. Mendel begins two years of careful trials before selecting twenty-two varieties of peas to test.

Mendel carefully pollinates seventy pea plants. He removes part of the plant called the stamen, which produces pollen, and applies the pollen to the stigma of a different pea plant. This process of cross-pollination allows Mendel to experiment with traits he sees in the various parent plants and determine how they can be replicated in the offspring.

An 1885 botanical illustration of a pea plant

He dries the peas until they turn to seeds. Looking at their seeds, he can easily see differences. Some of the seeds are wrinkled; some stay smooth. Mendel crosses wrinkled-seed peas with smooth-seed peas, yellow seeds with green, seeds from tall plants with those from short. He keeps meticulous records. He harvests, he plants, and he takes notes.

His second generation of peas have mixed inheritances: they are hybrid, which means they are the offspring of parents with different traits. He can hardly wait until the plants ripen. Then he carefully tabulates the results.

When he opens the pods of this first generation of hybrids, he discovers that all the peas—every one of them—produced smooth seeds. The wrinkling has totally vanished!

What about seed color? He has taken pollen from green- and yellow-seed plants and bred them. But in this first hybrid generation he finds only yellow seeds. What is going on? Why is one characteristic dominating completely? Why have others disappeared? What has happened to the wrinkling and the green color? Is there no averaging or mixing at all?

He now has the new, hybrid generation of smooth yellow-seed peas self-pollinate to produce the next pea generation. This time he gets both wrinkled and smooth pea seeds! The wrinkled-seed trait skipped a generation, but it has returned. The same has happened with the green seeds.

In breeding experiments, the first, or parental, generation is often represented by the letter P. Offspring are known as filial generations. The first set of offspring is called the F_1 generation. The F_2 generation is the offspring of the F_1 generation, and so on.

This is complicated, but Mendel is a statistician, so he keeps track of every pod. He harvests 7,324 peas in his F_2 generation. Of that crop, 5,474 produce smooth seeds and 1,850 produce wrinkled seeds. It is a ratio of just about three to one. And that ratio holds up for other characteristics, such as seed color (yellow/green), flower color (purple/white), and size (tall/dwarf).

Mendel keeps planting. His experiments soon involve "more than 10,000 carefully examined plants." What happens when he mates the third, F_3 generation?

The plants with wrinkled seeds produce only wrinkled-seed offspring. But those with smooth seeds are a complex lot:

one of every three smooth-seed plants produces only smooth-seed offspring. The other two produce both smooth and wrinkled seeds at a ratio of three to one.

Meanwhile, Darwin, at his comfortable home in Downe, England, follows up *Origin of Species* with a book examining the interrelation and evolution of orchids and the insects that pollinate them. He has also discovered the three-to-one ratio, but Darwin, who doesn't think mathematically, never grasps its importance.

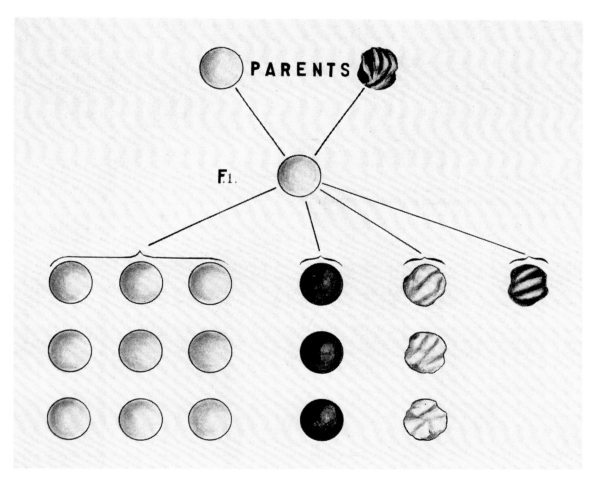

A diagram of some of Mendel's pea experiments

Smooth Peas, Wrinkled Peas

The thousands of pea plants that Mendel breeds show how a variety of characteristics change over time. Below, we look at how one trait—whether peas are wrinkled or smooth—changes after Mendel's cross-fertilization.

A stands for the smooth-pea trait, a for the wrinkled-pea trait—each trait coming from one of the parents. One trait, in this case smoothness, is dominant, meaning that if both traits are passed down to the same pea, the dominant trait, smoothness, will prevail.

Mendel takes pollen from one set of peas and uses it to fertilize the other. One set is purely smooth, the other purely wrinkled. The first generation is created by the offspring. What he finds is that hybrids that have mixed traits (Aa) produce offspring that have characteristics in a roughly 3:1 ratio—a dominant characteristic, in this case smoothness, will be the predominant characteristic in three of every four of the mixed-trait hybrids' offspring:

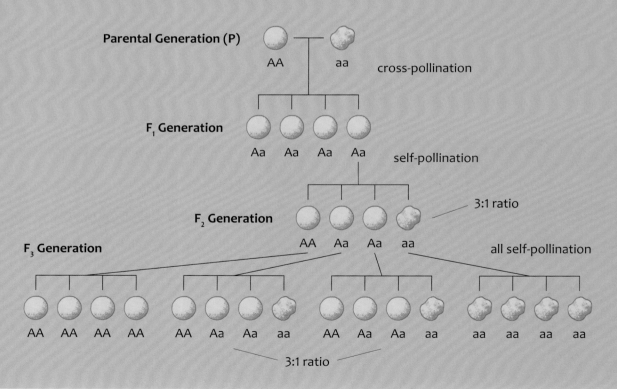

In a seven-year period (1856 to 1863), Mendel plants and tests nearly thirty thousand pea plants. His study of statistics has made him aware of the importance of big numbers—and that studies with larger test samples tend to be more accurate because they even out chance quirks that can show up in smaller groups.

This testing has led him to conclude that heredity, life's ability to pass on traits or characteristics, is controlled by inherited factors, and these factors behave in predictable ways.

Mendel coins the terms *recessive* and *dominant* to describe characteristics such as color or size or shape. Recessive factors—such as wrinkles in pea seeds—seem to disappear; when plants with wrinkled seeds are crossed with plants with smooth seeds, a dominant characteristic, they produce only smooth-seeded offspring. But the wrinkled-seed factor is just in hiding. It's recessive. In subsequent generations, recessive factors reappear, in a predictable mathematical pattern.

In 1865, Mendel describes his work in a scholarly paper, "Experiments on Plant Hybridization." He explains that he's figured out that inheritance of traits (whether in peas or, presumably, people) is determined by what he terms "factors" and that those factors are passed from one generation to the next in patterns that can be predicted and measured. No one has yet used statistics as he has to explain change in the natural world. Mendel reads the paper to the Brünn Society for the Study of Natural Science and describes numerical ratios that result from hybridization. His paper is published by the society and, as is the custom, sent to other scientific organizations in Europe and America.

Mendel sees that genes follow these three simple statistical principles:

1. Factors are inherited by descendants unchanged; we now call those factors "genes."

2. An individual inherits two factors for each trait, one factor from each parent. Only one is expressed.

3. A trait can be passed down to the next generation even if does not appear in the parent.

Because Mendel's brilliance is not widely recognized in his lifetime, his papers are burned after his death. Those that survive become rare and quite valuable as his contributions become apparent. In 1911, in a big cleanup at the Brünn Society for the Study of Natural Science, a soon-to-become-priceless manuscript written by Gregor Mendel is thrown into a trash can. A local high school teacher sees it, pulls it out of the trash, and puts it back into the society's files. Then, when Germany invades Czechoslovakia during World War II, a German botany professor takes it. Later he returns it to the files. After that, the Russians take over Czechoslovakia, and the paper disappears again. Half a century later, a monk in Prague sends it to a Mendel family member, a priest named Father Clemens.

Now the story gets complicated: the family says they own the paper (which has become very valuable); the Catholic Church says it belongs to them. Germany, the Czech Republic, and Austria also get involved, vying for what has become a treasure of scientific history.

The dispute is settled in 2012, and after years of negotiations, it is agreed the document will be displayed at the Mendel Museum, near the abbey in the Czech Republic where Mendel once lived.

Mendel writes to some well-known scientists, sending copies of his paper. He probably does not send a copy to Darwin. Darwin's enormous library does include a book with one page devoted to Mendel's pea experiments, but it's not clear if Darwin was aware of that particular page.

When Abbot Napp dies, Mendel is elected abbot by his peers; his days become filled with church work. Mostly he puts science aside, although he remains an avid meteorologist. In 1877, he urges the government of Moravia, the region where the abbey is located, to help local farmers make use of weather forecasting data, and he continues in later years to publish on that topic. And, according to biographer Robin Marantz Henig, "He collected good jokes the way Darwin collected barnacles, underlining the

A statue of Mendel that stands outside the Mendel Museum at Masaryk University in Brno, Czech Republic

best ones in the humor journal *Fliegende Blätter* ('Flying Leaves') to read to his brethren at the dining table."

When Mendel dies, in 1884, the people of Brünn grieve the loss of their kind, modest abbot. They have no idea that a great scientist has lived in their midst.

We began this chapter with two siblings, one with blue eyes and one with brown. Blue eyes are recessive, and brown eyes are dominant; although it's not quite that simple. With eye color in humans, several factors of inheritance are at work. Scientists will learn that and much more in the years to come, when Mendel's work provides a foundation for genetics, a science that has changed our world. ■

Treading a Primrose Path

Science is impossible without hypotheses and theories; they are the plummets with which we test the depth of the ocean of unknown phenomena and thus determine the future course to be pursued on our voyage of discovery.

—August Weismann

But, good my brother,
Do not, as some ungracious pastors do,
Show me the steep and thorny way to heaven,
Whiles, like a puffed and reckless libertine,
Himself the primrose path of dalliance treads.

—William Shakespeare, *Hamlet*

A butterfly among primroses, by the Belgian artist and botanist Pierre-Joseph Redouté

Primroses, a low-growing flowering plant native to northern Europe, explode with yellow, pink, or purple blossoms just as winter's chill retreats. Their timing and colors may be why the common primrose is a favorite of gardeners and poets and just about everyone who, after a long winter, is ready for flowers and warm weather.

In 1900, when Dutch botanist Hugo de Vries (1848–1935) treads a primrose path, it is not composed of the pretty one poets have in mind. De Vries, who is struggling to understand how heredity works, cultivates an exotic and showy primrose, an American native that sometimes grows to be five feet (1.5 meters) tall. Known as evening primrose, it was introduced into Europe around 1178 and eventually renamed *Oenothera lamarckiana* in honor of Lamarck, who died in 1829. This big primrose is not at all like the ground-hugging primrose used in British gardens. De Vries understands that when he finds "a strain of this beautiful species . . . growing on an abandoned field . . . a short distance from Amsterdam. Here it has escaped from a park and multiplied."

De Vries, who has reservations about Darwin's theory of natural selection, wants to prove or disprove it. He is not convinced of its importance. He quotes American botanist James Arthur Harris, who pithily commented that "natural selection may explain the survival of the fittest, but it cannot explain the arrival of the fittest."

As de Vries understands it, Darwinian evolution is too slow to explain nature's changes. Challenging Darwin, he cites examples of rapid change in nature. He sees the Dutch/American primrose plants as an example of rapid change. For no apparent reason, they may suddenly grow big heads and long stems. De Vries calls these unexpected changes "sports," or "mutations." And—this surprises him—he finds that the mutants don't mate with other primroses. Why not? De Vries doesn't know, but he realizes that they must be a new species, which he names *Oenothera gigas*. This is startling. With this primrose, nature seems to be creating new species, and doing it quickly.

Hugo de Vries in a 1918 portrait

De Vries has been a taxonomist—focusing on plant classification. Now he begins doing laboratory experiments that track generational change in the primrose plants; he keeps mathematical records of the results, eventually tracking roughly fifty-three thousand plants.

He comes to conclusions that are much like those of Gregor Mendel when he tracked peas numerically. "Attributes of organisms consist of distinct, separate and independent units," de Vries writes. In other words, and this is important: heredity seems to focus on "independent units" that carry traits. In 1889, de Vries publishes a book, *Intracellular Pangenesis*, in which he talks of the units, or "pangenes," that seem to determine inheritance. He even suggests that some of these units may cross lines between species. Years later, the term *pangene* will be shortened to *gene*.

At some point during this period, de Vries becomes aware of Mendel's earlier work, though accounts vary as to how he became aware of it and precisely when. But he realizes that he is not first with his discoveries. Still, when he publishes a paper on inheritance in a French journal, he makes no mention of Mendel. A German botanist, Carl Correns (1864–1933), who studied under an academic who had corresponded with Mendel, reads the paper and criticizes de Vries for ignoring Mendel's work. So, in March of 1900, de Vries reads both his paper and Mendel's at a meeting of a German botanical society.

One month later, Correns reads a paper of his own on the same subject before the same society's members. He too has experimented, found hereditary "units," read Mendel's paper, and understood that Mendel was first to make this discovery. Correns adds an insight: he has found that some traits are linked and remain together from generation to generation.

Correns doesn't realize that flower colors are determined by genes that carry instructions for producing pigments that color petals. But he is quite sure that traits like petal color are not random. There is a system at work in the colors in his garden, and he is trying to understand it.

Then, in June, an Austrian scientist named Erich von Tschermak (1871–1962) presents a paper at the same botanical society. He too has experimented with peas and found mathematical ratios in his results. When he researches previously published studies in the field and discovers Mendel's work, he gives credit where it is due.

These three biologists, all working in the same field, have verified Mendel's results and have seen hereditary units at work. They publicize their findings—and share Mendel's work more widely.

Suddenly everyone wants to know about Gregor Mendel. He has posthumously become a scientific celebrity. The units Mendel described are now being called determinants, biophores, factors, or particles of inheritance. But how do they determine inheritance? The evening primrose does not provide de Vries with the answers he had hoped for. That is because he doesn't know where to look.

Johannes Friedrich Miescher (1844–1895) does. Miescher is studying medicine at the University of Basel in Switzerland when he gets a bad case of typhoid fever; he drops out of school for a year.

Miescher graduates, but he gives up the idea of being a medical doctor. He switches to chemical research and is soon studying pus, that gross gunk that forms on healing wounds. He scrapes a steady supply of the stuff from used bandages he gets at a nearby hospital. Pus contains leucocytes, white blood cells.

Miescher uses chemical processes to isolate the center of each white blood cell—the nucleus. He soon has a lot of nuclei. Remember: this is the nineteenth century, and the cell has hardly been studied.

Swiss biologist Johannes Friedrich Miescher

When Miescher bathes the cells in alcohol, it removes fats. He treats what is left with an acid he gets from pig stomachs that contains pepsin, which destroys proteins. Meischer ends up with a fat-free, protein-free stringy glop, which he calls "nuclein" because he has found it in nuclei. We now call it DNA.

Meischer has no idea what he has discovered. Nor does anyone else. Four years later, in 1872, he finds nuclein in the sperm of salmon (which is easier to deal with than pus from hospital bandages).

He asks himself: If nuclein is in sperm, might it play a role in the reproduction process? If so, what is that role? Meischer doesn't know the answer to these questions. When he dies, at age fifty-one, he has no idea of the importance of his discovery.

The same year (1868) that Meischer discovers nuclein, Charles Darwin comes up with a theory he calls "pangenesis." Darwin realizes that his natural selection theory won't amount to much if no one can figure out how inheritance happens. According to his theory of pangenesis, tiny particles of inheritance, "gemmules," from diverse cells travel through a liquid in the body (maybe blood), heading for the reproductive organs (which hold eggs and sperm), where they direct the heredity process (however it might work).

Our primrose biologist, de Vries, is aware of Darwin's pangenesis idea. De Vries's 1889 book about the factors of inheritance calls those factors pangenes, after Darwin's theory.

Darwin believes there may be entities that are carriers of inheritance information. He should be considering Miescher's nuclein, but Darwin doesn't even know about Miescher's research.

A widely held idea is that inherited characteristics are carried in blood. This notion is expressed in the term *bloodlines* and in the expression "Blood will tell." Kings and queens are believed to have "royal blood."

Darwin's cousin Francis Galton (1822–1911) decides to test this blood idea with rigorous experiments on thirteen litters of rabbits. He injects blood from silver-gray rabbits into common field rabbits. Then he breeds them. Their babies all turn out to be field rabbits, and so does the next generation, with not a silver-gray among them.

Galton's experiment axes his cousin's theory. Darwin gets uncharacteristically angry and finally says if it isn't blood, it may be another bodily liquid that carries the gemmules. Galton does more experimenting; he can find no evidence of gemmules. Pangenesis, a briefly popular idea, has led nowhere.

August Weismann (1834–1914), a German biologist, decides to do some heredity testing himself. He's aware that unexpected differences may be essential if change is to happen in the life process, but they are not the norm in heredity. Most characteristics seem to get inherited over and over again.

No one is totally sure if acquired characteristics can be inherited, as Lamarck believed. Weismann wonders whether some acquired characteristics can cause unexpected changes and decides to do an experiment. He chops off the tails of thousands of rats—twenty generations of them—to see if any of the altered rats give birth to tailless babies. None do.

In 1883, in *Essays Upon Heredity*, Weismann says, "Heredity is brought about by the transference from one generation to another, of a substance with a definite chemical, and, above all, molecular constitution." He calls the

August Weismann, German biologist

substance a "determinant" and says it's present in all cells. But no one has uncovered the secrets of that determinant yet. That will be left to future generations of scientists. ■

Looking Ahead

At the beginning of this book, humanity's understanding of life was in a jumble. Then Carl Linnaeus began to sort creatures of the earth and sea into species. Linnaeus was followed by Charles Darwin, Alfred Russel Wallace, and others who put forth new ideas about how life evolves and changes. Gregor Mendel cataloged peas at his abbey, using numbers to show how traits pass down through generations. While many—including scientists—disputed these discoveries, our understanding of evolution rocketed forward, and the ideas shared by Darwin and Mendel continued to develop.

As this book ends, picture the nineteenth century's leading scientists at a conference; they are asking one another about how life works. They think they are close to finding answers, but they don't always look in the right places or ask the right questions. It's not their fault. Many of the answers they seek are hidden deep inside the cells that are the building blocks of all life-forms. Those cells are very tiny; no one has the tools yet to clearly see inside them.

An engraving showing twelve species of primates, including humans

Microscopes, and the technology that supports them, will get better—much better. Soon scientists will be able to see a world that has been invisible. They will see that there is a nucleus inside the cell and, within it, the building blocks of life.

For Further Reading

In this book, humans began to grapple with how life adapts and changes over time, and how traits are passed down by parents from generation to generation. Darwin is the most important person in the book. He and Abraham Lincoln (who share a birthday: February 12, 1809) are said to have had more books written about them than almost anyone else in history (which means there are many good books about Darwin that aren't in the list below).

To write a book, you need to read a lot of other ones. My husband, Sam, who is usually good-natured, sometimes feels overwhelmed by how many books surround us. He is quite sure they have found a way to procreate (meaning to produce new books) and that books will soon take over our apartment and we will have to move into the hallway. Here are some books that were particularly helpful to me as I researched and wrote this one:

Allen, Garland, and Jeffrey Baker. *Biology: Scientific Process and Social Issues*. Bethesda, MD: Fitzgerald Science Press, 2001. Provides some scholarly insights into the background of modern biology.

Bowler, Peter J. *Evolution: The History of an Idea*. Berkeley, CA: University of California Press, 2009.

Bryson, Bill. *A Short History of Nearly Everything*. New York: Broadway Books, 2004. This author goes wherever his curiosity leads and then looks for explanations of how things work or how they evolved. A well-researched and interesting read.

Bulmer, Michael. *Francis Galton: Pioneer of Heredity and Biometry*. Baltimore, MD: Johns Hopkins University Press, 2003. Galton, a leading scientific thinker in his time, got a lot wrong, which is often part of the process of discovery.

Butler, Samuel. *The Collected Works*. Charleston, SC: BiblioBazaar, 2008.

Clements, Jonathan. *Darwin's Notebook: The Life, Times, and Discoveries of Charles Robert Darwin*. Philadelphia: Running Press, 2009. Darwin's writings—personal and scientific—presented as a journal. A good book for beginning to understand Darwin's legacy.

Darwin, Charles. *Autobiographies*. Edited by Michael Neve and Sharon Messenger. London: Penguin Classics, 2002. This small book includes carefully chosen fragments of Darwin's writing. It's a good place to start and find out if you want to read more.

————. *Charles Darwin: His Life Told in an Autobiographical Chapter, and in a Series of His Published Letters.* Edited by Francis Darwin. London: John Murray, 1892.

————. *Geological Observations on the Volcanic Islands and Parts of South America Visited during the Voyage of H.M.S.* Beagle. London: Smith, Elder, 1844.

————. *The Life and Letters of Charles Darwin.* Edited by Francis Darwin. 2 vols. London: John Murray, 1887.

————. *On the Origin of Species.* Edited by Joseph Carroll. Toronto: Broadview Press, 2003. This book is ranked among the most influential works ever. I originally read a copy that belonged to my father, but this paperback edition and others are widely available.

————. *The Voyage of the* Beagle. New York: Collier, 1909. Originally published in 1839 as *Narrative of the Surveying Voyages of His Majesty's Ships* Adventure *and* Beagle, *Journal and Remarks: Describing Their Examination of the Southern Shores of South America, and the* Beagle's *Circumnavigation of the Globe,* this is the book that made Darwin famous.

Davies, Roy. *The Darwin Conspiracy: Origins of a Scientific Crime.* London: Golden Square, 2008. According to Davies, Darwin stole his big idea and got away with that theft because he was part of the British establishment. He makes a serious case for the charge.

Eldredge, Niles. *Reinventing Darwin: The Great Debate at the High Table of Evolutionary Theory.* New York: Wiley, 1995. Eldredge, with his colleague Stephen Jay Gould, came up with a controversial theory that evolution proceeds in fits and starts rather than as a process of slow, even change.

Fuller, Randall. *The Book That Changed America: How Darwin's Theory of Evolution Ignited a Nation.* New York: Viking, 2017. How Darwin influenced scientific thinking in America.

Gelbart, Nina Rattner. *Minerva's French Sisters: Women of Science in Enlightenment France.* New Haven, CT: Yale University Press, 2021. Tells the story of half a dozen French women whose scientific work during the Enlightenment was largely forgotten.

Gopnik, Adam. *Angels and Ages: A Short Book about Darwin, Lincoln, and Modern Life.* New York: Knopf, 2009. Gopnik, who writes regularly for the *New Yorker*, says, "We live in a society based on two foundations—scientific reasoning and democratic politics." In this book, he takes on the superstar of each discipline. London's *Guardian* calls it "the perfect introduction to their lives."

Grant, K. Thalia, and Gregory B. Estes. *Darwin in Galápagos: Footsteps to a New World*. Princeton, NJ: Princeton University Press, 2009. In this book, modern biologists, considering Darwin as a forerunner, take readers on a tour of the Galápagos Islands.

Harari, Yuval Noah. *Sapiens: A Brief History of Humankind*. New York: Vintage, 2015. Beginning fourteen billion years ago with the big bang, when our universe is believed to have begun, Harari tells the story of the evolution of life on Earth.

Henig, Robin Marantz. *The Monk in the Garden: The Lost and Found Genius of Gregor Mendel, the Father of Genetics*. Boston: Houghton Mifflin, 2000. An informative book about Mendel.

Jackson, Patrick Wyse. *The Chronologers' Quest: The Search for the Age of the Earth*. Cambridge, England: Cambridge University Press, 2006. The story of an interesting scientific venture.

Lyell, Charles. *Sir Charles Lyell's Scientific Journals on the Species Question*. Edited by Leonard G. Wilson. New Haven, CT: Yale University Press, 1970. Interesting notes from Lyell, a scientist who was a mentor to Darwin.

McCalman, Iain. *Darwin's Armada: Four Voyages and the Battle for the Theory of Evolution*. New York: Norton, 2009.

Moorehead, Alan. *Darwin and the* Beagle. New York: Harper & Row, 1969. Gorgeous illustrations, handsome design, and lyrical text.

Oldstone, Michael B. A. *Viruses, Plagues, and History: Past, Present, and Future*. Rev. ed. Oxford: Oxford University Press, 2010. This scholarly book details how plagues can change the world.

Osterhammel, Jürgen. *Unfabling the East: The Enlightenment's Encounter with Asia*. Translated by Robert Savage. Princeton, NJ: Princeton University Press, 2018. A look at the broader cultural connections across the world, and in Asia in particular, that helped shape the Enlightenment era.

Quammen, David. *Natural Acts: A Sidelong View of Science and Nature*. Rev. ed. New York: Norton, 2008. Essays on science by an eloquent writer focusing on questions that Darwin asked.

———. *The Tangled Tree: A Radical New History of Life*. New York: Simon & Schuster, 2018. Perceptive thoughts on Darwin's meaning today.

Silvertown, Jonathan, ed. *99% Ape: How Evolution Adds Up*. London: Natural History Museum, 2008. Scientists comment on evolution in this illustrated book.

Stott, Rebecca. *Darwin and the Barnacle*. New York: Norton, 2004. This book focuses on Darwin's years studying barnacles and why they are essential in understanding one of the world's greatest scientists.

———. *Darwin's Ghosts: The Secret History of Evolution*. New York: Spiegel & Grau, 2012. A book full of stories and surprises, mostly about amazing life scientists who came before Darwin.

Tort, Patrick. *Charles Darwin: The Scholar Who Changed Human History*. London: Thames and Hudson, 2001. A small, beautifully illustrated book packed with information.

Uglow, Jenny. *The Lunar Men: Five Friends Whose Curiosity Changed the World*. New York: Farrar, Straus, and Giroux, 2002. The story of some dynamic thinkers laying foundations for the industrial world, told with eloquence.

White, Michael, and John Gribbin. *Darwin: A Life in Science*. New York: Dutton, 1995. This book about Darwin is intended for a general audience.

Wootton, David. *The Invention of Science: A New History of the Scientific Revolution*. New York: HarperCollins, 2015. A serious but readable book that covers the major sciences and also strays into literature and history. Read about Copernicus, Tycho Brahe, Thomas Digges, and William Shakespeare.

Source Notes

Introduction

p. 1: "change the way people think": quoted in Joseph Epstein, "A Philosophe in Full: Denis Diderot's Enlightenment," *Claremont Review of Books*, Fall 2019, https://claremontreviewofbooks .com/a-philosophe-in-full/; my translation.

p. 1: "All things must be . . . anyone's feelings": quoted in Tim Blanning, *The Romantic Revolution: A History* (New York: Modern Library, 2012), 6.

p. 1: "in natural science . . . observation": Carol von Linné, *Linnaeus' Philosophia Botanica*, trans. Stephen Freer (Oxford: Oxford University Press, 2003), 307.

p. 2: "Dare to Know!": Immanuel Kant, "An Answer to the Question: What Is Enlightenment?" trans. Ted Humphrey (Indianapolis: Hackett, 1992), n3, https://www.nypl.org/sites/default/files/kant _whatisenlightenment.pdf.

p. 2: "cause lies not . . . from another": ibid., 1.

p. 2: "have courage . . . understanding!": ibid.

p. 2: "Around the mid-eighteenth . . . periphery": Osterhammel, 115.

p. 2: "all men by nature are equal": John Locke, *Second Treatise of Government*, ed. C. B. Macpherson (Indianapolis: Hackett, 1980), 31.

p. 2: "Man was born . . . in chains": Jean Jacques Rousseau, *The Social Contract and Discourses*, trans. G. D. H. Cole (New York: Dutton, 1950), 3.

p. 4: "men are born . . . in rights": "Declaration of the Rights of Man – 1789," Avalon Project, Yale Law School, Lillian Goldman Law Library, https://avalon.law.yale.edu/18th_century/rightsof.asp.

p. 5: "like cows at market": quoted in Lisa Beckstrand, *Deviant Women of the French Revolution and the Rise of Feminism* (Madison, NJ: Fairleigh Dickinson University Press, 2009), 101.

Chapter 1

p. 11: "If you do not know . . . lost too": von Linné, 169.

p. 11: Learning is not . . . diligence": Abigail Adams to John Quincy Adams, March 20, 1780, Founders Online, National Archive, https://founders.archives.gov/documents/Adams/04-03-02-0240.

p. 12: "God created, Linnaeus organized": *Deus creavit, Linnaeus disposuit*: D. H. Stoever, *The Life of Charles Linnaeus*, trans. Joseph Trapp (London: E. Hodson, 1794), frontispiece; as frequently translated.

p. 13: "one of the origins . . . for humanity": "Linnaeus and Race," Linnean Society of London, https://www.linnean.org/learning/who-was-linnaeus/linnaeus-and-race.

p. 15: "I ask you . . . I certainly know of none": quoted in Jane Spencer, *Writing about Animals in the Age of Revolution* (Oxford: Oxford University Press, 2020), 30.

p. 15: "If I were to call man ape . . . the rules of science": quoted in John Gribbin, *The Scientists: A History of Science Told Through the Lives of Its Greatest Inventors* (New York: Random House, 2004), 219.

Chapter 2

p. 17: "Buffon's work . . . closer to the truth'": Michael Shermer, *In Darwin's Shadow: The Life and Science of Alfred Russel Wallace; A Biographical Study on the Psychology of History* (New York: Oxford University Press, 2002), 103.

p. 17: "The grand workman of nature is Time": Georges-Louis Leclerc, comte de Buffon, *Buffon's Natural History*, ed. James Smith Barr, vol. 6 (London: H. D. Symonds, 1807), 24.

p. 19: "by every educated person in Europe": Ernst Mayr, *The Growth of Biological Thought: Diversity, Evolution, and Inheritance* (Cambridge, MA: Belknap/Harvard University Press, 1982), 330.

p. 21: "Instead of 50,000 years . . . ceased to burn": Georges-Louis Leclerc, comte de Buffon, *Buffon's Natural History*, ed. James Smith Barr, vol. 10 (London: H. D. Symonds, 1807), 114.

p. 21: "He was the first person . . . raised by anybody": Mayr, 335.

p. 22: "There is no absolute essential . . . latter to the vegetable": Georges-Louis Leclerc, comte de Buffon, *Buffon's Natural History*, ed. James Smith Barr, vol. 2 (London: H. D. Symonds, 1797), 263.

p. 22: "Lines of separation . . . vegetables, nor minerals": Georges-Louis Leclerc, *Buffon's Natural History*, ed. James Smith Barr, vol. 3 (London: H. D. Symonds, 1807), 166.

p. 24: "In America, therefore . . . Old Continent": quoted in Todd Timmons, *Makers of Western Science: The Works and Words of 24 Visionaries from Copernicus to Watson and Crick* (Jefferson, NC: McFarland, 2012), 86.

p. 25: "'Our land is more . . . grass of these plains'": quoted in Basil Johnston, *Honour Earth Mother* (Lincoln, NE: University of Nebraska Press, 2003), xv.

p. 25: "Who in France, after all, would know?": Bryson, 80.

p. 26: "recorded information . . . enslavement": "Enlightenment Influence: Racism in Jefferson's *Notes on the State of Virginia*, 1781," Monticello website, Thomas Jefferson Foundation, https://www.monticello.org/slavery/paradox-of-liberty/thomas-jefferson-liberty-slavery/a-society -dependent-on-slavery/racism-in-jefferson-s-notes-on-the-state-of-virginia/.

p. 26: "During the dinner . . . nature degenerated'": Thomas Jefferson, *The Writings of Thomas Jefferson*, ed. Paul Leicester Ford, vol. 3, 1781–1784 (New York: Putnam, 1894), n.168.

p. 27: "Those of the other side were remarkably diminutive": ibid.

p. 27: "the incognitum, or mammoth": Thomas Jefferson, *The Writings of Thomas Jefferson*, ed. H. A. Washington, vol. 8 (New York: Riker, Thorne, 1854), 287.

p. 28: "It is well known . . . all terrestrial beings": ibid., 286, 289.

p. 28: "Such is the economy . . . to be broken": ibid., 296.

p. 29: "It is easier . . . from heaven": quoted in Brooks Mather Kelley, *Yale: A History* (New Haven, CT: Yale University Press, 1974), 136.

Chapter 3

p. 31: "The Lunar men . . . know today": Uglow, xiii.

p. 31: "The improved steam engine . . . inorganic world": David Christian, *Maps of Time: An Introduction to Big History* (Berkeley, CA: University of California Press, 2004), 421.

p. 32: "a little philosophical laughing": quoted in Tom Blaney, *The Chief Sea Lion's Inheritance: Eugenics and the Darwins* (Leicester, UK: Troubador, 2011), 23.

p. 32: "I hate piddling": Josiah Wedgwood, *The Life of Josiah Wedgwood*, vol. 2 (London: Hurst and Blackett, 1866), 331.

p. 32: "surprise the World with wonders": quoted in Uglow, xvii.

p. 32: "Lord! what invention . . . troop of philosophers": quoted in H. W. Dickinson, *Matthew Boulton* (Cambridge: Cambridge University Press, 2010), 187.

p. 33: "I shall never forget . . . to have,—Power'": ibid., 73.

p. 33: "The linking of science . . . contemporary Scotland": Uglow, 33.

p. 34: "I hope this will give . . . of woods": quoted in Jean-Pierre Poirier, *Lavoisier: Chemist, Biologist, Economist*, trans. Rebecca Balinski (Philadelphia: University of Pennsylvania Press, 1996), 52.

p. 35: "At times it would . . . colony of Scotland": ibid., 34.

p. 35: "What ran through . . . material decency": quoted in John H. Lienhard, *The Engines of Our Ingenuity: An Engineer Looks at Technology and Culture* (Oxford: Oxford University Press, 2000), 91.

p. 35: "Dr. Darwin upon the road": quoted in Anna Seward, *Memoirs of the Life of Dr. Darwin: Chiefly During His Residence in Lichfield, with Anecdotes of His Friends, and Criticisms on His Writings* (London: J. Johnson, 1804), 152.

p. 37: "I absolutely nauseate Darwin's poem": quoted in Martin Priestman, *The Poetry of Erasmus Darwin: Enlightened Spaces, Romantic Times* (Burlington, VT: Ashgate, 2013), 224.

p. 37: "Dr. Darwin . . . man in Europe": ibid., 226.

p. 39: "a living filament . . . with intervening web": Erasmus Darwin, *Zoonomia; Or, The Laws of Organic Life*, vol. 1 (Boston: Thomas & Andrews, 1809), 377.

p. 39: "use and disuse": A. M. Winchester, "Genetics," in *Encyclopaedia Britannica* (online ed., 2022), https://www.britannica.com/science/genetics#ref936953.

p. 39: "Would it be . . . world without end?": Erasmus Darwin, 1:397.

p. 39: "Organic Life beneath . . . and wing": Erasmus Darwin, *The Temple of Nature: Or, the Origin of Society* (London: Jones, 1825), 14–15.

p. 41: "He was much . . . closed during summer": Charles Darwin, *Charles Darwin's "The Life of Erasmus Darwin,"* ed. Desmond King-Hele (Cambridge: Cambridge University Press, 2003), 43.

Chapter 4

p. 43: "What nature does . . . is situated": Jean Baptiste Pierre Antoine de Monet de Lamarck, *Zoological Philosophy*, trans. Hugh Samuel Roger Elliott (Cambridge: Cambridge University Press, 2011), 109.

p. 43: "Linnaeus and Cuvier . . . old Aristotle": Charles Darwin, *Life and Letters*, 2:427.

p. 46: "the marvelous operation that nature executes on all organized bodies": quoted in Gelbart, *Minerva's French Sisters*, 234.

p. 49: "How was it overlooked . . . of the globe?": Georges Cuvier, *Discourse on the Revolutions of the Surface of the Globe and the Changes Thereby Produced in the Animal Kingdom* (Philadelphia: Carey and Lea, 1831), 36.

p. 50: "It took them . . . another like it": quoted in Arthur L. Donovan, "Antoine Lavoisier: The French Revolution and Lavoisier's Execution," in *Encyclopaedia Britannica* (online ed., 2022), https://www.britannica.com/biography/Antoine-Lavoisier/The-French-Revolution-and-Lavoisiers-execution.

p. 51: "I only say . . . of the globe": Georges Cuvier, *Essay on the Theory of the Earth*, 5th ed. (London: T. Cadell, 1827), 113.

p. 52: "anatomical marvel": quoted in Nina Rattner Gelbart, "Everything But the Stench," *Lapham's Quarterly*, June 7, 2021, https://www.laphamsquarterly.org/roundtable/everything-stench.

p. 53: "soft inheritance": quoted in Thomas Hayden, "What Darwin Didn't Know," *Smithsonian Magazine*, February 2009, https://www.smithsonianmag.com/science-nature/what-darwin-didnt-know-45637001/.

p. 53: "disagreeable circumstances . . . we are made": quoted in Gelbart, *Minerva's French Sisters*, 191.

Chapter 5

p. 55: "In the nineteenth century . . . the world": Shelley Emling, *The Fossil Hunter: Dinosaurs, Evolution, and the Woman Whose Discoveries Changed the World* (New York: St. Martin's Griffin, 2011), 38.

p. 55: "It would not . . . up Holborn Hill": Charles Dickens, *Bleak House* (London: Bradbury and Evans, 1852), 1.

p. 57: "so thoroughly . . . this kingdom": quoted in Emling, 89–90.

p. 58: "She sells sea shells on the seashore": quoted in Katherine Bouton, "Tale of an Unsung Fossil Finder, in Fact and Fiction," *New York Times*, February 1, 2010, https://www.nytimes.com/2010/02/02/science/02scibooks.html.

p. 64: "9,000 living species of birds, compared with 4,100 species of mammals": John Noble Wilford, "But Will It Fly?" *New York Times*, January 25, 1998, https://www.nytimes.com/1998/01/25/books/but-will-it-fly.html.

p. 65: "The crowds lead . . . of the collection": quoted in Robert McCracken Peck, "The Art of Bones," *Natural History Magazine*, https://www.naturalhistorymag.com/features/11340/the-art-of-bones?page=2.

Chapter 6

p. 67: "A fool . . . in his life": quoted in Maria Edgeworth, *The Life and Letters of Maria Edgeworth*, ed. Augustus J. C. Hare (Boston: Houghton Mifflin, 1895), 1:22.

p. 67: "I love fools' experiments. I am always making them": quoted in James T. Costa, "The Impish Side of Evolution's Icon," *American Scientist*, March–April 2018, https://www.americanscientist.org/article/the-impish-side-of-evolutions-icon.

p. 68: "I was interested at this early age in the variability of plants!": Charles Darwin, *Charles Darwin: His Life Told*, 6.

p. 68: "a monstrous fable": ibid.

p. 68: "I have been . . . a naughty boy": ibid.

p. 68: "Nothing could have . . . strictly classical": ibid., 8.

p. 68: "Especial attention . . . never do well": ibid., 9.

p. 68: "I was considered . . . all your family'": ibid.

p. 68: "the intense . . . gave me": ibid.

p. 69: "used to sit . . . of the school": ibid.

p. 69: "I was allowed . . . books on chemistry": ibid., 11.

p. 69: "I tried to . . . had this taste": ibid., 6.

p. 70: "I have been most shockingly . . . novels at once": Charles Darwin, *Origins: Selected Letters of Charles Darwin, 1822–1859*, ed. Frederick Burkhardt, rev. ed. (Cambridge: Cambridge University Press, 2008), 8.

p. 71: "incredibly dull": Charles Darwin, *Charles Darwin: His Life Told*, 14.

p. 71: "the proper way to do birds": Charles Waterton, *Wanderings in South America*, 3rd ed. (London: B. Fellowes, 1836), 158.

p. 72: "He gave me . . . intelligent man": Charles Darwin, *Charles Darwin: His Life Told*, 53.

p. 72: "I spent many hours in conversation at his side": quoted in "John Edmonstone," Africh Royale, https://africhroyale.com/john-edmonstone/.

p. 72: "any effect on me": Charles Darwin, *Charles Darwin: His Life Told*, 13.

p. 73: "I . . . saw two very bad operations . . . a long year": ibid., 12.

p. 73: "I did not . . . in the Bible": ibid., 17.

p. 73: "No pursuit at . . . which was lost": *Charles Darwin, Life and Letters*, 1:43.

p. 74: "captured by C. Darwin, Esq.": ibid.

p. 75: "stirred up in . . . Natural Science": ibid., 1:55.

Chapter 7

p. 79: "It must have . . . the moon": Charles Lyell, *Principles of Geology* (London: John Murray, 1830), 3:5.

p. 79: "Seeing every . . . on this earth": Charles Darwin, *Voyage of the* Beagle, 400.

p. 82: "On the shores . . . firm conglomerate": Charles Darwin, *Geological Observations on the Volcanic Islands, Visited during the Voyage of H.M.S.* Beagle (London: Smith, Elder, 1844), 21–22.

p. 82: "The dust falls in . . . eyes": Charles Darwin, *Voyage of the* Beagle, 15.

p. 82: "no less than sixty-seven different organic forms": ibid.

p. 82: "knows many species . . . South America": ibid.

p. 82: "Delight is a . . . me with admiration": ibid., 22.

p. 82: "The noise from . . . experience again": ibid.

p. 83: "the perfect dust storm": "Understanding Earth: The Journey of Dust," NASA, https://eospso.nasa.gov/sites/default/files/publications/TheJourneyofDust_508.pdf, 2.

p. 83: "millions of tons . . . Deserts": ibid.

p. 83: "white haze": ibid., 4.

p. 83: "I tried to find . . . down the trunk": ibid.

p. 85: "I shall have a large box to send very soon to Cambridge": Charles Darwin, *Charles Darwin: His Life Told*, 134.

p. 85: "You have done wonders": Charles Darwin and J. S. Henslow, *Darwin and Henslow: The Growth of an Idea; Letters 1831–1860*, ed. Nora Barlow (Berkeley, CA: University of California Press, 1967), 66.

p. 86: "I have seen . . . not quite clean": Charles Darwin, *Voyage of the* Beagle, 499–500.

p. 86: "blood boil, yet heart tremble": Charles Darwin, *Voyage of the* Beagle, 527.

p. 87: "You cannot imagine . . . these weeks": Richard Darwin Keynes, ed., *The Beagle Record: Selections from the Original Pictorial Records and Written Accounts of the Voyage of H.M.S.* Beagle (Cambridge: Cambridge University Press, 2012), 61.

p. 88: "confirmed Darwin's belief . . . essential humanity": Adrian Desmond and James Moore, *Darwin's Sacred Cause: Race, Slavery and the Quest for Human Origins* (Boston: Houghton Mifflin Harcourt, 2009), 26.

p. 88: "savages": Darwin used this term frequently in Charles Darwin, *Voyage of the* Beagle.

p. 89: "They were delighted . . . to our boats" and "every woman . . . uneasy at this": Charles Darwin, *Voyage of the* Beagle, 238.

p. 90: "mysterious grandeur . . . mass of forest": ibid., 226.

p. 90: "The atmosphere . . . anywhere else": ibid.

p. 92: "a field of snow-white salt": ibid., 33.

p. 92: "How surprising it . . . soda and lime": ibid.

p. 92: "We have a little . . . lakes of brine": ibid., 78.

p. 92: "Well may we affirm . . . support organic beings": ibid., 33.

p. 92: "how every character . . . slow degrees": ibid., 109.

p. 92: "A canoe, with a little flag flying": ibid., 244.

p. 92: "Every soul on board . . . last time": ibid., 245.

p. 92: "I do not now doubt . . . his own country": ibid.

p. 94: "The earth . . . crust over a fluid": ibid., 322.

p. 94: "as if a thousand ships had been wrecked": ibid., 321.

p. 95: "We can scarcely . . . solid land": Charles Darwin, *Narrative of the Surveying Voyages of His Majesty's Ships* Adventure *and* Beagle (London: Henry Colburn 1839), 3:380.

p. 95: "a little world within itself": ibid., 77.

p. 95: "imps of darkness": quoted in Charles Darwin, *Charles Darwin's* Beagle *Diary*, ed. Richard Darwin Keynes (Cambridge: Cambridge University Press, 1988), 353.

p. 97: "He had grown . . . more as a sailor": Moorehead, 211.

Chapter 8

p. 99: "As Darwin now conceived it . . . existence": Janet Browne, *Charles Darwin*, vol. 2, *The Power of Place* (New York: Knopf, 1996), 7.

p. 99: "Evolution by natural selection . . . human sciences": Robert M. Young, "Science and the Humanities in the Understanding of Human Nature," *On Line Opinion*, June 15, 2000, https://www.onlineopinion.com.au/view.asp?article=1171&page=3.

p. 101: "The charm . . . any other country": Charles Darwin, *Correspondence*, 2:324.

p. 103: "Species have . . . does not exist": William Whewell, *History of the Inductive Sciences*, vol. 3 (London: John W. Parker, 1837), 576.

p. 103: "Each species changes": quoted in Michael Ruse and Robert J. Richards, eds., *The Cambridge Companion to the "Origin of Species"* (Cambridge: Cambridge University Press, 2009), 50.

p. 104: "my theory": ibid., 113.

p. 104: "descent with modification": ibid., 199.

p. 105: "whole fabric totters & falls": Charles Darwin, *Notebook C: Transmutation of Species* (1838), ed. John van Wyhe, Darwin Online, 76, http://darwin-online.org.uk/content/frameset?itemID=CUL -DAR122.-&viewtype=text&pageseq=1.

p. 105: "But Man—wonderful Man is an exception" and "He is no exception": ibid., 77.

Chapter 9

p. 109: "In science . . . idea first occurs": Francis Darwin, "Francis Galton," *Eugenics Review* 6, no. 1 (April 1914), 9.

p. 109: "Mr. Darwin has . . . no further go!!!": Wallace, *My Life*, 1:372–373.

p. 110: "Through reading . . . in the house": ibid., 1:17.

p. 111: "I begin to feel . . . collection": ibid. 1:256.

p. 111: "I should like . . . origin of species": ibid., 1:256–257.

p. 111: "I have a rather more favourable . . . attend to": ibid., 1:254.

p. 112: "shining out like a mass of brilliant flame": Alfred Russel Wallace, *Travels on the Amazon* (London: Ward, Lock, 1911), 152.

p. 113: "I was to begin . . . incident of my life": Wallace, *My Life*, 1:336.

p. 113: "Every species has . . . closely-allied species": ibid., 1:335.

p. 113: "almost unimaginable . . . new species": Shermer, 14.

p. 113: "progressive development of plants and animals": Wallace, *My Life*, 1:254.

p. 115: "I wish you . . . cited and understood": Charles Darwin, *Correspondence*, 6:89.

p. 115: "With respect . . . array of facts": ibid., 6:100

p. 115: "a few days ago": ibid., 6:387.

p. 116: "The problem then . . . died out)": Wallace, 1:361.

p. 116: "It then occurred . . . would be explained": ibid., 1:361–362.

p. 116: "Even his terms stand as heads of my chapters": Charles Darwin, *Life and Letters*, 116.

p. 116: "one of the greatest . . . history of science": Davies, xix.

p. 116: "vindicated from accusations of deceit": John Van Wyhe and Kees Rookmaaker, "A New Theory to Explain the Receipt of Wallace's Ternate Essay by Darwin in 1858," *Biological Journal of the Linnean Society*, 105, no. 1 (January 2012), 249, https://academic.oup.com/biolinnean/article/105/1/249/2452581.

p. 117: "I can plainly . . . similar conclusions": quoted in Alfred Russel Wallace, *Infinite Tropics: An Alfred Russel Wallace Anthology*, ed. Andrew Berry (London: Verso, 2002), 35.

Chapter 10

p. 119: "Truth is born . . . do not occur": quoted in Alma E. Cavazos-Gaither and Carl C. Gaither, eds., *Gaither's Dictionary of Scientific Quotations* (New York: Springer, 2012), 2576.

p. 119: "The publication of . . . thought of that!'": Charles Darwin, *Life and Letters*, 2:197.

p. 120: "The year which has passed . . . brilliant innovation": quoted in "160th Anniversary of the Presentation of 'On the tendency of Species to form Varieties,'" Linnean Society website, July 1, 2018, https://www.linnean.org/news/2018/07/01/1st-july-2018-160th-anniversary-of-the-presentation-of-on-the-tendency-of-species-to-form-varieties.

p. 120: "thirty-odd nonplussed fellows": quoted in John Bellamy Foster, *The Return of Nature: Socialism and Ecology* (New York: Monthly Review Press, 2021), 219.

p. 121: "Natural selection . . . daring theory" and "based on . . . three inferences": Ernst Mayr, *What Evolution Is* (New York: Basic Books, 2001), 115.

p. 122: "Not many days . . . made upon me": Alfred Newton, "Early Days of Darwinism," *Macmillan's Magazine*, 57, February 1888, 244.

p. 122: "contained a perfectly . . . months past": ibid.

p. 122: "I never doubted . . . was so simple": ibid.

p. 124: "Who trusted God . . . against his creed": Alfred, Lord Tennyson, "In Memoriam," *The Complete Works of Alfred, Lord Tennyson* (New York: Frederick A. Stokes, 1891), 135.

p. 124: "It is interesting . . . acting around us": Charles Darwin, *Origin of Species*, 429.

p. 125: "Darwin's bulldog": quoted in Sylvio G. Codella, "Not Just Darwin's Bulldog," *Bioscience*, 50, no. 10 (October 1, 2000), https://academic.oup.com/bioscience/article/50/10/914/234051.

p. 126: "survival of the fittest": Herbert Spencer, *The Principles of Biology*, rev. ed. (London: Williams and Norgate, 1898), 1:290.

p. 127: "stand at the summit of civilisation": Charles Darwin, *The Descent of Man, and Selection in Relation to Sex*, 2nd ed. (London: John Murray, 1896), 141.

p. 127: "When the views . . . in natural history": Charles Darwin, *Origin of Species*, 489.

Chapter 11

p. 129: "When a theory . . . attention to it": François Jacob, *The Logic of Life: A History of Heredity* (Princeton, NJ: Princeton University Press, 1993), 12.

p. 129: "Mendel's genius . . . different angle": Henig, 6.

p. 131: "May the might . . . come after me": ibid., 17–18.

p. 136: "more than 10,000 carefully examined plants": quoted in Alain F. Corcos and Floyd V. Monaghan, *Gregor Mendel's Experiments on Plant Hybrids: A Guided Study* (New Brunswick, NJ: Rutgers University Press, 1993), 72.

p. 141: "He collected . . . the dining table": Henig, 167.

Chapter 12

p. 143: "Science is impossible . . . voyage of discovery": quoted in Frederic W. Putnam, ed., *Proceedings from the American Association for the Advancement of Science*, August 1891 (Salem, MA: Salem Press, 1892), 303.

p. 143: "But good . . . of dalliance treads": William Shakespeare, *Hamlet*, ed. Burton Raffel (New Haven, CT: Yale University Press, 2003), 30.

p. 144: "a strain of . . . park and multiplied": Hugo de Vries, *Species and Varieties: Their Origin by Mutation*, ed. Daniel Trembly MacDougal (Chicago: Open Court, 1905), 27.

p. 144: "Natural selection . . . of the fittest": ibid., 825–826.

p. 146: "Attributes of organisms . . . independent units": Hugo de Vries, *The Mutation Theory*, 2 vols., trans. J. B. Farmer and A. D. Darbishire (Chicago: Open Court, 1909), 1:3.

p. 149: "Heredity is brought . . . molecular constitution": August Weismann, *Essays Upon Heredity*, eds. Edward B. Poulton, Selmar Schönland, and Arthur E. Shipley (Oxford: Clarendon, 1889), 168.

Bibliography

Allen, Garland, and Jeffrey Baker. *Biology: Scientific Process and Social Issues*. Bethesda, MD: Fitzgerald Science Press, 2001.

Bolles, Edmund Blair. *Galileo's Commandment: An Anthology of Great Science Writing*. New York: W. H. Freeman, 1997.

Bowler, Peter J. *Evolution: The History of an Idea*. Berkeley, CA: University of California Press, 2009.

Bryson, Bill. *A Short History of Nearly Everything*. New York: Broadway Books, 2004.

Bulmer, Michael. *Francis Galton: Pioneer of Heredity and Biometry*. Baltimore, MD: Johns Hopkins University Press, 2003.

Butler, Samuel. *The Collected Works*. Charleston, SC: BiblioBazaar, 2008.

Clements, Jonathan. *Darwin's Notebook: The Life, Times, and Discoveries of Charles Robert Darwin*. Philadelphia: Running Press, 2009.

Darwin, Charles. *Autobiographies*. Edited by Michael Neve and Sharon Messenger. London: Penguin, 2002.

———. *Charles Darwin: His Life Told in an Autobiographical Chapter, and in a Series of His Published Letters*. Edited by Francis Darwin. London: John Murray, 1892.

———. *The Correspondence of Charles Darwin*. Edited by Frederick Burkhardt and Sydney Smith. 30 volumes. Cambridge: Cambridge University Press, 1985–2022.

———. *Geological Observations on the Volcanic Islands and Parts of South America Visited during the Voyage of H.M.S. Beagle*. London: Smith, Elder, 1844.

———. *The Life and Letters of Charles Darwin*. Edited by Francis Darwin. 2 vols. London: John Murray, 1887.

———. *On the Origin of Species by Means of Natural Selection*. London: John Murray, 1859.

———. *The Voyage of the Beagle*. New York: Collier, 1909. First published in 1839 as *Narrative of the Surveying Voyages of His Majesty's Ships* Adventure *and* Beagle, *Journal and Remarks: Describing*

Their Examination of the Southern Shores of South America, and the Beagle's *Circumnavigation of the Globe* by Henry Colburn (London).

Davies, Roy. *The Darwin Conspiracy: Origins of a Scientific Crime*. London: Golden Square, 2008.

Dyson, Freeman. *Origins of Life*. Rev. ed. Cambridge: Cambridge University Press, 1999.

Eldredge, Niles. *Reinventing Darwin: The Great Debate at the High Table of Evolutionary Theory*. New York: Wiley, 1995.

Ferris, Timothy. *The Whole Shebang: A State-of-the-Universe(s) Report*. New York: Simon & Schuster, 1997.

Fuller, Randall. *The Book That Changed America: How Darwin's Theory of Evolution Ignited a Nation*. New York: Viking, 2017.

Gee, Henry. *A (Very) Short History of Life on Earth: 4.6 Billion Years in 12 Pithy Chapters*. New York: St. Martin's, 2021.

Gelbart, Nina Rattner. *Minerva's French Sisters: Women of Science in Enlightenment France*. New Haven, CT: Yale University Press, 2021.

Gopnik, Adam. *Angels and Ages: A Short Book about Darwin, Lincoln, and Modern Life*. New York: Knopf, 2009.

Grant, K. Thalia, and Gregory B. Estes. *Darwin in Galápagos: Footsteps to a New World*. Princeton, NJ: Princeton University Press, 2009.

Harari, Yuval Noah. *Sapiens: A Brief History of Humankind*. New York: Vintage, 2015.

Henig, Robin Marantz. *The Monk in the Garden: The Lost and Found Genius of Gregor Mendel, the Father of Genetics*. Boston: Houghton Mifflin, 2000.

Jackson, Patrick Wyse. *The Chronologers' Quest: The Search for the Age of the Earth*. Cambridge, England: Cambridge University Press, 2006.

King-Hele, Desmond. *Erasmus Darwin: A Life of Unequalled Achievement*. London: Giles de la Mare, 1999.

Lyell, Charles. *Sir Charles Lyell's Scientific Journals on the Species Question*. Edited by Leonard G. Wilson. New Haven, CT: Yale University Press, 1970.

McCalman, Iain. *Darwin's Armada: Four Voyages and the Battle for the Theory of Evolution*. New York: Norton, 2009.

Mesler, Bill, and H. James Cleaves II. *A Brief History of Creation: Science and the Search for the Origin of Life*. New York: Norton, 2016.

Milner, Richard. *Darwin's Universe: Evolution from A to Z*. Oakland, CA: University of California Press, 2009.

Moorehead, Alan. *Darwin and the* Beagle. New York: Harper & Row, 1969.

Morus, Iwan Rhys, ed. *The Oxford Illustrated History of Science*. Oxford: Oxford University Press, 2017.

Oldstone, Michael B. A. *Viruses, Plagues, and History: Past, Present, and Future*. Rev. ed. Oxford: Oxford University Press, 2010.

Osterhammel, Jürgen. *Unfabling the East: The Enlightenment's Encounter with Asia*. Translated by Robert Savage. Princeton, NJ: Princeton University Press, 2018.

Quammen, David. *Natural Acts: A Sidelong View of Science and Nature*. Rev. ed. New York: Norton, 2008.

———. *The Tangled Tree: A Radical New History of Life*. New York: Simon & Schuster, 2018.

Shapiro, James A. *Evolution: A View from the 21st Century*. Upper Saddle River, NJ: FT Press Science, 2011.

Shermer, Michael. *Why Darwin Matters: The Case Against Intelligent Design*. New York: Henry Holt, 2006.

Silvertown, Jonathan, ed. *99% Ape: How Evolution Adds Up*. London: Natural History Museum, 2008.

Singer, Charles. *A Short History of Scientific Ideas to 1900*. Oxford: Oxford University Press, 1959.

Stott, Rebecca. *Darwin and the Barnacle*. New York: Norton, 2004.

———. *Darwin's Ghosts: The Secret History of Evolution*. New York: Spiegel & Grau, 2012.

Strager, Hanne. *A Modest Genius: The Story of Darwin's Life and How His Ideas Changed Everything*. Foreword by Sarah Darwin. Translated by Graham Timmins. CreateSpace, 2016.

Tomaselli, Sylvana. *Wollstonecraft: Philosophy, Passion, and Politics*. Princeton, NJ: Princeton University Press, 2022.

Tort, Patrick. *Charles Darwin: The Scholar Who Changed Human History*. London: Thames and Hudson, 2001.

Uglow, Jenny. *The Lunar Men: Five Friends Whose Curiosity Changed the World*. New York: Farrar, Straus, and Giroux, 2002.

Wallace, Alfred Russel. *My Life: A Record of Events and Opinions*. 2 vols. London: Chapman & Hall, 1905.

Ward, Peter, and Joe Kirschvink. *A New History of Life: The Radical New Discoveries about the Origins and Evolution of Life on Earth*. New York: Bloomsbury, 2015.

Weiner, Jonathan. *The Beak of the Finch: A Story of Evolution in Our Time*. New York: Vintage, 1995.

White, Michael, and John Gribbin. *Darwin: A Life in Science*. New York: Dutton, 1995.

Wootton, David. *The Invention of Science: A New History of the Scientific Revolution*. New York: HarperCollins, 2015.

Zimmer, Carl. *The Tangled Bank: An Introduction to Evolution*. Greenwood Village, CO: Roberts, 2010.

Image Credits

Index

natural selection and, 8, 126

portrait, *108–109*

publication, 119

Sarawak Law, 113

species variations, 114–115

transmutation theory and, 111

travels of, 112–113

Vestiges of the Natural History of Creation, 111

Ward, Peter, 63

Waterhouse, George, 100

Waterton, Charles, 71

Watt, James, 33

workroom, *30–31*

Wedgwood, Josiah, 32, *41*, 69

Wedgwood pottery, 32

Weismann, August, 143, 149

Whewell, William, 102–103

Wilford, John Noble, 64

Wollstonecraft, Mary, 6

women, Enlightenment. *See* Anning, Mary; Baret, Jeanne; Bihéron, Marie Marguerite; Shelley, Mary Wollstonecraft; Thiroux d'Arconville, Geneviève; Wollstonecraft, Mary

Wood, William, 70

Wright, Joseph, 119

Yaghan people, 89–90

Young, Robert M., 99

Zoology of the Voyage of H.M.S. Beagle, The (Charles Darwin), 79, 90, 93

Zoonomia (Erasmus Darwin), 35, 39

JOY HAKIM is the best-selling author of A History of US, a ten-volume history of the United States, as well as the Story of Science series and the first book in the Discovering Life's Story series, *Biology's Beginnings*. She has worked as a teacher, journalist, and editor and lives in Maryland.